Elements in World Englishes
edited by
Edgar W. Schneider
University of Regensburg

LANGUAGE IDEOLOGIES AND IDENTITIES ON FACEBOOK AND TIKTOK

A Southern Caribbean Perspective

Guyanne Wilson
University College London

Shaftesbury Road, Cambridge CB2 8EA, United Kingdom

One Liberty Plaza, 20th Floor, New York, NY 10006, USA

477 Williamstown Road, Port Melbourne, VIC 3207, Australia

314–321, 3rd Floor, Plot 3, Splendor Forum, Jasola District Centre, New Delhi – 110025, India

103 Penang Road, #05–06/07, Visioncrest Commercial, Singapore 238467

Cambridge University Press is part of Cambridge University Press & Assessment, a department of the University of Cambridge.

We share the University's mission to contribute to society through the pursuit of education, learning and research at the highest international levels of excellence.

www.cambridge.org
Information on this title: www.cambridge.org/9781009494809

DOI: 10.1017/9781009350808

When citing this work, please include a reference to the DOI 10.1017/9781009350808

First published 2024

A catalogue record for this publication is available from the British Library.

ISBN 978-1-009-49480-9 Hardback
ISBN 978-1-009-35076-1 Paperback
ISSN 2633-3309 (online)
ISSN 2633-3295 (print)

Additional resources for this publication at www.cambridge.org/Guyanne

Language Ideologies and Identities on Facebook and TikTok

A Southern Caribbean Perspective

Elements in World Englishes

DOI: 10.1017/9781009350808
First published online: May 2024

Guyanne Wilson
University College London

Author for correspondence: Guyanne Wilson, guyanne.wilson@ucl.ac.uk

Abstract: This Element examines the ways in which Caribbean content creators use elements of Caribbean Englishes and Creoles in their performances of identity in image macro memes and TikTok videos. It also examines the ideologies that underlie these performances. The data comprises memes from Trinidadian Facebook pages, as well as videos by Guyanese, Barbadian, and Trinidadian TikTokers, and was analysed using the multimodal method designed by Kress. For meme makers, identity is understood as a system of distinction between in-groups and out-groups, and language and other semiotic features, notably emojis, are used to distinguish Trinidadians from other nationalities, and groups of Trinidadians from one another. TikTokers establish their Caribbean identity primarily through knowledge of lexis, but this works in concert with other linguistic features to create authentic identities. Social media content is underpinned by the tension between the acceptance and rejection of standard language ideologies.

This element also has a video abstract: www.cambridge.org/Wilson

Keywords: World Englishes on social media, multimodality, indexicality, language and identity, language ideologies

ISBNs: 9781009494809 (HB), 9781009350761 (PB), 9781009350808 (OC)
ISSNs: 2633-3309 (online), 2633-3295 (print)

Contents

1 Setting the Scene 1

2 Identities and Ideologies in Facebook Memes 23

3 Identity and Ideologies in TikTok Videos 46

4 Indexing Identity, Enregistering Ideology 72

References 80

1 Setting the Scene

1.1 Introduction

The digital turn in arts and humanities scholarship has led to increased attention being given to language use on the internet and computer-mediated communication. Such research has focussed, crucially, on how online spaces, particularly social media sites, can be used to conduct linguistic research (e.g. Androutsopolous 2017); how changes in written language forms have accompanied the increased use of online communication; how processes of bi- and multilingualism, such as code-switching, take place online (e.g. Androutsopolous 2015); and how written resources such as the hashtag have been adapted into the work of identity in online spaces (e.g. Zappavigna 2011). Widespread global internet use, particularly among younger segments of populations, perhaps coupled with the idea that online spaces upset traditional national borders, has meant that, while some economically and demographically larger countries are better represented in the research, there are few localities that are completely absent from scholarly discourse.

This Element focusses on social media use by content creators from the English-using Caribbean with an emphasis on Barbados, Guyana, and Trinidad. These territories were chosen because the Englishes spoken here are linked historically (see Holm 1986: 15; Winford 1997: 247), and contemporary migration patterns within the Caribbean mean that economic and social competition are accompanied by intense language contact. Records of internet and social media usage in the Caribbean show relatively high levels of engagement with digital communications across the region. The data collection platform Statista reports that, for the year 2022, 84.6 per cent of the population of Barbados used social media, compared to 67.1 per cent of the population of both Guyana and Trinidad and Tobago.[1] The same report shows that Facebook is the main social networking platform used across the region, accounting for as much as 77.19 per cent of all social media usage in Trinidad and Tobago. Though no other platform sees as much traffic as Facebook, the use of Instagram, TikTok, and Snapchat has risen since 2020 and is predicted to remain stable until 2027. Beyond phatic communicative needs, Caribbean netizens use social media to enhance health education provision (Cathala et al. 2022), spread information about the movement for reparations (Esposito 2018), and explore and exchange ideas about beauty and haircare with other netizens (Maynard and Jules 2021). However, despite the role that language must play in all these

[1] We Are Social, and Hootsuite, and Data Reportal (January 26, 2022). Percentage of population using social media in Latin America and Caribbean as of February 2022, by country [Graph]. In *Statista*. www.statista.com/statistics/454805/latam-social-media-reach-country/.

interactions, few studies have undertaken to explore how language is used in them.

Studies of language on social media in the English-using Caribbean have, to date, been focussed on written language use particularly in emails, blogs, and online chat forums (e.g. Moll 2015; Mühleisen 2022), with the earliest interest in online language focussed on orthographic representations of Caribbean Creoles (Hinrichs and White-Sustaita 2011) and how these are linked to attitudes towards, in this case, Jamaican Creole and it being made distinct from English. While online communication does favour written language, social media is a particularly heightened multimodal space, and content creators on social media draw not only on writing but also on speech, song, and static and dynamic visual effects, very often simultaneously. This Element goes beyond written language to explore the ways in which Caribbean social media users perform aspects of their identity in two understudied genres of online communication: image macro memes circulated on Facebook and TikTok videos. Furthermore, the current work considers the ways in which ideologies about language use in the Caribbean, both in digital and in analogue spaces, are reinforced or renegotiated in the online sphere. Although there exist a number of social media platforms, Facebook and TikTok will be the focus of this Element due to their popularity in the region. The specific research questions guiding this Element are as follows:

- How are specific phonological, lexical, grammatical, and pragmatic features of Caribbean Englishes and Creoles exploited in the creation of Caribbean identities by content creators from Barbados, Guyana, and Trinidad?
- What non-linguistic elements are drawn upon in the development of Caribbean identities online?
- Identity is a broad concept, encompassing notions of gender, class, and region. What specific aspects of Caribbean identity are highlighted through language use online?
- How are attitudes and ideologies surrounding language use in the region reinforced, or challenged, in social media content?

The rest of this section contains an overview of language in Barbados, Guyana, and Trinidad, focussing on shared features across the varieties as well as language ideologies and identities in each of the countries. I also discuss key literature on language use on social media, focussing on memes and TikTok videos, though the latter form has not been widely researched. Owing to practical constraints, I focus particularly on work that has looked at Caribbean and diasporic communities. In the remaining subsections of Section 1, I then describe how data was collected and the method of multimodal analysis and discuss the ethics of working with social media data. In Section 2, the first of two case studies is discussed. It looks at identities and ideologies in image macro memes, focussing on memes produced by Trinidadian content creators and circulated via Facebook. The analysis is primarily linguistic with some consideration of other semiotic features of the memes. Section 3 is the second case study, in which the language of TikTokers from Barbados, Guyana, and Trinidad is examined. The three TikTokers studied are involved in the production of parallel, competing content, and so their videos offer a unique insight into how language on social media differentiates groups from one another. In the fourth and final section of this Element, I attempt to situate my findings about memes and TikTok videos within broader discourses of indexicality and enregisterment and hope to demonstrate thereby one way in which the sister disciplines of World Englishes and sociolinguistics can better communicate with each other.

1.2 Language in the Caribbean

English-using Caribbean territories such as Barbados, Guyana, and Trinidad and Tobago are characterised by the presence of at least two, coexisting language varieties: an English-lexifier Creole on the one hand, which here will be referred to as Creole, and a local variety of standardised English on the other, which here will be referred to as English. Creoles are contact phenomena, the result of English coming into contact with the languages of the enslaved people kidnapped from Africa and brought to the Caribbean between the seventeenth and nineteenth centuries. The relationship between Creole and English is best understood with regard to the concept of the Creole continuum (De Camp 1971; but for a thorough exploration on continuum in the three territories discussed here, see Winford 1997). This concept acknowledges three vaguely fixed points that are 'not discrete varieties, but a continuous transition between creole and standard poles' (Rickford 1987: 18). At one end of the continuum is the basilect, which is regarded as the variety that is the most distant from English (Bickerton 1975: 24), and which contains the most influence from African languages (Alleyne 1971: 180). At the other extreme of the continuum is the acrolect, the local variety of standardised English (Bickerton 1975). At the middle point of the continuum is the mesolect, and at points along the continuum there is considerable mixing, so there is no real way of saying where one variety ends and another begins. This difficulty has led to some scholars, notably Winer (2009) in her *Dictionary of the English/Creole of Trinidad and Tobago*, adopting the term English/Creole as a way of acknowledging the vague boundaries between varieties.

The notion of the Creole continuum cannot be applied equally to the linguistic situation across Caribbean countries. As Winford (1997: 236) notes, the linguistic situation in Barbados and Trinidad is similar. On both islands, there is a 'fairly uniform intermediate [C]reole used in both rural and urban areas' as well as a local variety of standardised English. Moreover, there is evidence for the presence of features in the rural Creoles that are absent in urban varieties. For Guyana, in contrast, Winford notes the presence of three distinct varieties: a basilectal rural creole, a mesolectal creole spoken in urban areas, and a local variety of standardised English.

1.2.1 Features of Caribbean Creoles

There exist several thorough general descriptions of Caribbean Englishes and Creoles (e.g. on Barbadian phonology, Blake 2008; on the phonology of Trinidadian and Tobagonian Englishes, Youssef and James 2008; on the grammar of the same, James and Youssef 2008; and on Guyanese Creole, Rickford 1987), but this section highlights only those features relevant for the subsequent discussion, based on an overview of Caribbean Englishes presented in Lacoste (2013). In terms of consonants, Caribbean English/Creole may be characterised by TH-stopping, that is, the realisation of English dental fricatives as stops, so that words such as *thin* and *then* become [tɪn] and [dɛn]. Furthermore, English consonant clusters are often reduced word finally (or alternatively do not exist in the Creole underlying forms). This means than *send* and *sent* may be pronounced as a homophone, [sɛn]. Caribbean Creoles share with non-standardised varieties of English the realisation of verbal [ɪŋ] as [ɪn] in words like *jumping*. Barbadian speech is rhotic in post-vocalic contexts and is further distinguished by the glottalisation of voiceless stops in syllable-final position (Blake 2008: 314), so that *part* and *park* are potential homophones, both being realised as [pa:rʔ]. Guyanese speech shows variable rhoticity, but Trinidadian speech is generally non-rhotic except in borrowings from Indic languages, such as *kurma* (a sweet). One consonantal feature that Youssef and James (2008: 517–518) list for Trinidad but which Lacoste overlooks is the palatalisation of the velar consonants /k/ and /g/, which may be realised as [kj] and [gj], particularly by rural Indo-Trinidadians. Rickford (1987) also attests the presence of this feature in Guyanese.

The key feature of Caribbean English/Creole vowels is the monophthongisation of diphthongs in the FACE and GOAT lexical sets, so that words in those sets are realised as [e:] and [o:] respectively. In Barbadian and Guyanese English/Creole LOT may be realised as [ɑ] (with [a] also possible in Guyanese), and THOUGHT may be realised as [ɑ:] (with [a:] also possible in Guyanese). Perhaps the most stereotypical feature of Barbadian pronunciation is the realisation of the PRICE vowel as [ʌɪ], in which the first element of the diphthong is raised and backed in comparison to the realisation of the same vowel in other varieties of English. In Guyanese English/Creole, PRICE and CHOICE may merge in [aɪ].

Turning to grammar, the principal differences between Caribbean English/Creole and other varieties lie in the verb phrase and the noun phrase. Verbs typically are unmarked for both third-person singular -s and past tense -ed, so that constructions such as *The boy like to walk* and *He walk up the hill yesterday* are plausible. Moreover, English copula forms typically do not occur before predicative adjectives (e.g. *The girl funny*) or in progressive constructions (e.g. *The girl laughing at the joke*). In the noun phrase, plurals may be unmarked or else marked by the attributive *–(an) dem*, producing either *I pick five mango* or *I eat the mango dem*. Furthermore, possessor–possessed relationships are marked through adjacency, as in *The child toy fall on the floor*.

It is important to note that, given the continuum along which language varieties in the Caribbean exist, it is very rarely the case that speakers employ any of the above-mentioned features categorically, and there is variation along sociolinguistic categories such as socio-economic background and ethnicity, as well as according to register. For example, Winford's (1978) work on variation in Trinidad reports stratified distribution of [ð] and [θ] versus [d] and [t] by social class and by level of formality, with a general pattern of greater fricative realisation among speakers of the highest social classes in their most careful speech (with some hypercorrect behaviour by middle-class speakers). Likewise, Rickford (1987: 73) finds that speakers from the estate (working) class use basilectal pronominal forms more than non-estate class speakers in Guyana.

1.2.2 Language, Identity, and Ideology in the Caribbean

In their discipline-defining work on acts of identity, Le Page and Tabouret-Keller (1985) argue that people model their talk like that of the groups or individuals with whom they wish to be associated and interpret the shared features defining dialects of English as the result of continuous interaction and solidified group identity. Generally it is claimed that, where Caribbean Creoles are spoken alongside a standardised variety of English, Creole varieties also become important vehicles of identity.

Blake (1997: 170) argues that Creole in Barbados has been co-opted as a symbol of national unity, so that the 'renegotiation of identity towards nationhood plays a part in the vernacular not being highly stigmatized, to the extent that it is used as an effective mode of communication by blacks and whites alike on radio, television and in print'. At the same time, ideologies surrounding language use may result in the stigmatisation of Creole. Haynes (1982: 73) shows that urban Barbadians reported favouring British English over local varieties, though for rural respondents this result was reversed, and subsequent work by Fenigsen (2003: 461) finds that little had changed. English continued to be linked to intelligence and social mobility, while Creole bore connotations of plantation labour and was associated with a lack of education and professionalism, despite its connotations of local authenticity. In her 2009 dissertation, Belgrave reports that British English was rated favourably by participants in her matched guise and acceptability judgement tasks, often being viewed as 'proper' English.

An important aspect of identity throughout the Caribbean, but especially in Guyana and Trinidad, is ethnicity. In the post-emancipation period, both territories saw the arrival of indentured labourers from India to replace the newly freed African people, and, today, Indo-Guyanese and Indo-Trinidadians account for the majority population in both territories. In Guyana, language and identity have been linked to ethnicity, urban–rural distinctions, and social class. Rickford (1987) documents a number of structural features that distinguish Indo and Afro-Guyanese from each other. These include the devoicing of word-final /z/ and the realisation of /p/ as [f] (Rickford 1987: 159), as well as the use of the object marker *um* (Rickford 1987: 116–118). Sidnell (1999) builds on Rickford's earlier work, examining how pronominal usage varies with gender in a rural Indo-Guyanese community and showing how the use of basilectal pronominal forms is employed more widely by males in the community. However, although Guyana was the focus of much early work in Caribbean sociolinguistics, research on language in Guyana has been relatively sparse in more recent times.

Finally, Youssef (2004: 44) notes that, in Trinidad and Tobago, Creole is the 'language of solidarity [and] national identity', and research examining attitudes and ideologies in Trinidad in particular has shown growing awareness and acceptance of Creole in different spheres, though this is hardly uniform. For instance, Winford (1976) documents negative attitudes towards Creole among trainee teachers, but Mühleisen's (2001) follow-up study shows improved attitudes among a comparable group. Still, this should not be taken as evidence for broad acceptance of Creole; Deuber and Leung (2013) and Meer et al. (2019) both illustrate that standardised Trinidadian accents enjoy greater prestige in both media and education contexts and that American- and British-influenced speech is still viewed rather favourably. Moreover, Trinidadian society remains divided by race, and Indo- and Afro-Trinidadians differentiate themselves from each other linguistically. Leung and Deuber (2014: 16–17) show that Indo-Trinidadian women have a higher mean pitch and a wider pitch range than their Afro-Trinidadian counterparts and that listeners falsely judge Indo-Trinidadian speakers to be Afro-Trinidadian when their pitch is lowered mechanically. From a perceptual perspective, Stell (2018: 129) reports that varieties spoken by Indo-Trinidadians are associated with Central Trinidad and garner derogatory labels such as ‘Bush Indian talk’ or ‘coolie jargon’. These prior works have focussed on language in offline settings but raise questions as to how ethnic identity is performed in staged performances such as TikTok videos, and how attitudes and ideologies surrounding language and ethnicity are reproduced in social media content.

1.3 Language and Social Media

Memes are the ultimate form of text and visual modes combined. Shifman (2014: 41) defines internet memes, here simply memes, as ‘(a) a group of digital items sharing common characteristics of content, form, and/or stance, which (b) were created with awareness of each other and (c) were circulated, imitated, and/or transformed via the Internet by many users’. He makes a distinction between memes and virals, which he says are a single cultural unit, such as a video, picture, or other related content, that is spread via social media (p. 55). Critically for this distinction, virals are single instantiations; there is no further manipulation of the image or text to create further content. Memes, on the other hand, exist in many forms. Thus, Figure 1 is, in Shifman’s definition, a viral. It shows an image of a membership shopping centre, PriceSmart, that has been manipulated to read ‘Outsmart’ by the content creator and was shared on several platforms, including the Facebook page Stinkhtt. The image was created

Figure 1 Outsmart (Source: Stinkhtt)

following a scandal involving PriceSmart inaccurately withdrawing funds from members' bank accounts and, though it is circulated in this context, no other manipulations of the PriceSmart logo exist.

In contrast, Figures 2(a) and (b) are examples of manipulations of the Judgmental Volturi meme. The original image was taken from the film *Twilight: New Moon* and shows the vampire characters on a marble balcony looking down. Several instantiations of the meme exist, and it has come to be used to parody members of a society who are better off and look down on others.[2] In Figure 2(a), those looking down are members of the Trinidadian society who have access to electricity during a nationwide blackout. In Figure 2(b), the image is further manipulated, and the vampires' faces are replaced with those of prominent Trinidadian politicians – the prime minister, the minister of finance, and the minister of tourism – who are accused of asking people to make sacrifices while they themselves live lavish lives at the expense of the taxpayer. Memes often begin their lives as virals (Shifman 2014: 58), and, in this Element, I will not make a distinction between the two, since this distinction does not have any bearing on the analysis.

Memes here are limited to image macros, 'image[s] with captioned texts' (Wiggins 2019: 38). Their memetic character rests on three factors. First, they begin as stand-alone artefacts that, second, are created, changed within specific cultural and social contexts, and circulated by individuals participating in online digital culture where they, third, are perceived as having been purposefully

Figure 2 Manipulations of the Judgmental Volturi meme: (a) elite with electricity; (b) elite politicians.

[2] See *Judgemental Volturi* meme (2016), Know Your Meme website, posted by A. Walker. https://knowyourmeme.com/memes/judgmental-volturi.

produced and, as a result, are purposefully consumed (Wiggins 2019: 40). Moreover, Denisova (2019: 3) notes that memes are not fixed but, in the processes of change and re-creation, are 'interactive aesthetic artefacts that provide a snapshot of the immediate tendencies of culture and public discourse' and which 'change shape, style and size through mutation'. This is seen very clearly in Figure 2(b), where the meme is a reaction to statements made by the government following the reading of the budget, in which citizens were told to make sacrifices.

Previous research on internet memes has shown that memes are employed for a number of functions. Their primary function is to entertain, but memes have become central to the ways in which politics is discussed and public opinion is circulated 'in situations of oppression and crises, collective identification, and togetherness' (Mortensen and Neumayer 2021: 2369). For example, Unuabonah et al. (2021) look at Nigerian memes circulated in response to the Covid-19 pandemic in which posters criticise the Nigerian government's response to the crisis and the ensuing strain on public health and the food supply. They show how the creators of memes employ a range of semiotic and rhetorical devices, particularly humour, irony, and parody, to criticise government (in-)action and comment on the effects of the pandemic on Nigerian society.

As part of the participatory culture that characterises Web 2.0 environments, the identification work done through memes is not limited to their creators. Indeed, Yus (2018) underscores the importance of sharing memes, an action which implies a level of identification with the meme's content both for the sharer and for the receiver. Elsewhere, Chau (2021) examines the ways in which the persona of the fake American-born Chinese (ABC) woman, and her way of speaking, are enregistered in image macro memes and the discourses surrounding them. One key way in which this is done is via collaborative stylisation, in which 'the poster and commenters draw on a common set of discursive resources to stylize [ABC speech] together' (Chau 2021: 606).

Beyond memes, much online content creation comprises videos, particularly those on YouTube and, more recently, TikTok. Schneider (2016) explores the potential of YouTube as a source of data in the study of World Englishes. He identifies two main types of potentially useful videos on the platform: metalinguistic clips and natural clips. Schneider (2016) suggests that metalinguistic clips could be used to study aspects of language attitudes and performances, as seen in Bhatia's (2020) examination of code-switching in the vlogs of an Indo-British YouTuber, which shows how she uses English to symbolise her globalised, make-up artiste persona and Hindi to underscore her sustained identification as Indian. Natural clips can be used to carry out descriptions of varieties of English, for example of the phonological features of a given variety, as Zähres (2021) has demonstrated in using YouTube to describe phonological features of Namibian English. TikTok is a newer platform than YouTube, founded some eleven years after YouTube was launched. TikTok clips can also be divided into these two categories, though Ilbury (2023) argues that the staged nature of TikTok videos makes them a locus for stylised language performance and shows how Multicultural London English is co-opted in the creation the #Roadman character on TikTok. In the current Element, the TikToks used generally fall into Schneider's metalinguistic category, though there are elements of stylisation present.

Beyond memes, research on language in computer-mediated communication has focussed on written language, and particularly language use on Twitter and in the comments sections of Facebook and YouTube. Such comments sections often give important insights into the beliefs about language use and attitudes to different varieties, which may even be at odds with those reported in more conventional forms of data. For example, Leung (2017) explores metadiscourses surrounding the NURSE vowel in YouTube discussions of soca performances, and shows how, in this space, speakers whose language is otherwise the focus of ridicule are able to exercise linguistic agency. Elsewhere, Stuka (2023) has used Facebook comments to garner insights about the attitudes Barbadians hold towards American and British Englishes in particular. She also uses her corpus of Facebook comments to explore the spelling orientations by Barbadian writers. Mohammed and Thombre (2017) consider the pragmatic functions of posting on the Facebook pages of Indo-Trinidadian radio stations and conclude that greetings, requests, and inspirational messages left by commenters serve to reinforce both their Indo-Trinidadian and broader Indian diasporic identities.

One key feature of written language on social media is the use of code-switching and code-mixing. Shakir (2023) looks at the forms and functions of code-switching between Urdu and Pakistani English in different genres of writing on social media. He finds that code-switching is especially prevalent in Twitter posts, Facebook status updates, new media blogs, and comments sections (Shakir 2023: 52) and identifies several discursive functions that code-switching plays, such as emphasising arguments or the use of Urdu tags. Elsewhere, Kathpalia (2023) has shown how the mixing of Hindi and English in tweets about a James Bond film by Indian Twitter users highlights the way in which Western and Indian cultures come into contact. Kathpalia's study also highlights the ways in which code-switching and code-mixing can be used for both comedic and satiric effect – with Hindi–English mixing in her study being used to undermine conservative censorship laws.

Considerable attention has also been given to online interactions emerging in diaspora communities. These works highlight the importance of language in reasserting national identity in diasporic contexts and show how notions of prestige from the home country are not necessarily transplanted to a new environment. For example, Honkanen's (2020) work on the Nairaland corpus examines the range of linguistic resources Nigerian Americans have available to them (African American Vernacular English, Nigerian English, Nigerian Pidgin, and various Nigerian languages) and shows how, in particular, Nigerian Pidgin is mobilised as a resource for marking authentic Nigerian identity. In this way, Nigerian Pidgin loses some of the negative prestige it faces among Nigerians in Nigeria. Similarly, Moll (2015) finds that basilectal forms of Jamaican Creole, which, like Nigerian Pidgin, are stigmatised in Jamaica, are used in what Moll calls Cyber Jamaican to index Jamaican-ness. Finally, Mühleisen's (2022) study of an online forum for Trinbagonians in California finds that posters employ a number of Trinidadian English Creole features, particularly lexical and grammatical features, as well as spelling mirroring Trinidadian pronunciation, to index their Trinidadian identities. Moreover, through demonstrating knowledge of ongoing issues in Trinidad, they can make claims to membership. Though there is considerable interest in social media data produced in diaspora settings, there are no parallel studies for social media content generated within the Caribbean.

Another important aspect of computer-mediated communication is the emoji, 'a small digital image or icon used to express an idea, emotion, etc., in electronic communications' (*Oxford English Dictionary*). Emojis are critical elements of phatic emotive content in computer-mediated communication and, far from being decorative, are often crucial to conveying meaning. In the context of World Englishes, Honkanen and Mueller (2021) probe the ways in which surprise is expressed in Nairaland and find that representation of surprise through the shocked emoji accounts for nearly a quarter of all expressions of surprise in their corpus. Moreover, they report that the shocked emoji has a high probability of being used in concert with language expressing negative sentiments, in contrast to the sad emoji, which most often co-occurs with emotional language in English.

1.4 Researching Memes and TikTok Videos

In order to examine how Caribbean social media content reflects and reproduces identities and ideologies, data in the form of memes and videos was collected from Facebook and TikTok. This section describes the process of data collection and analysis and discusses some of the main issues surrounding the ethics of conducting research with social media data.

There are crucial differences between Facebook and TikTok in terms of popularity and user demographics. Facebook is by far the most popular social media site in the Caribbean, and indeed Facebook use has been the subject of the foundational social media research on the region (e.g. Sinanan 2017). However, the increasing popularity of TikTok among American users has led to scholars in other fields considering Facebook and TikTok use in the Caribbean alongside each other (e.g. Smith and Short 2022), and this will also be the case in the current Element. Facebook and TikTok are, of course, inherently different platforms – Facebook is primarily based on written language, with accompanying visual content, though it is also possible to produce video content. TikTok is primarily a video site, though interactions through likes and comments are similar to those of the older platform. However, cross-posting, that is, posting of content from one social media platform to another, seems to be a common practice. Moreover, it is often the case that influencers post the same content on more than one platform.

Facebook and TikTok users can be differentiated principally on the basis of their age. Among adult American social media users, TikTokers are usually aged 18–29, while Facebook use is reported in all demographic categories (18–29, 30–49, 50–64, over 65). These figures come with two important caveats. The first is that they refer to American usage, and similar, fine-grained analysis is not available for the Caribbean. Secondly, they refer to overall usage, but there are very different ways of engaging on social media: creating original content, sharing content created by others, and interacting with posts and posters via comments and likes. This information is not available.

1.4.1 Data Collection

The memes corpus comprises 200 memes collected between October 2019 and December 2022 from public Facebook pages: Trini Bakkanal; Trinidad is not a real place; We are Trinis; Penal Poet; Stinkhtt; and Trinis Be Like. Since the meme analysis is limited to identity-making and ideologies in Trinidadian English/Creole, only Facebook groups that overtly aligned themselves to Trinidad were included. Within these groups, only memes that referred to language were included, with memes often making reference to a specific linguistic feature. Reference to language could be phonological, lexical (including idioms), grammatical, or discoursal. For instance, Figure 3 refers to the Trinidadian idiomatic expression *wake up dead* (to die in one's sleep), while the meme in Figure 4 presents a stereotypical pronunciation. This is represented through eye dialect spellings (*kumar* for [kurmə] in Figure 4).

Figure 3 Wake up dead (Credit: *LWmemes*)

Figure 4 Kumar not kurma (Credit: Trinis Be Like)

Although language-based memes are common on Trinidadian Facebook sites, they do not appear to occur more frequently than memes that address other aspects of Trinidadian society such as politics, sport, or cultural practices, though these are not included in the analysis.

The memes had three basic sources. The first source was memes based on internet memes in wide circulation such as the *Woman Yelling at Cat* meme (Figure 3). In the *Woman Yelling at Cat* meme, a woman, held back by her friend, shouts something accusatorily to the cat, who hisses a response. Typically, in this meme, the woman's contribution is taken to be inaccurate or ridiculous, and the cat's contribution as logical and correct (though there are exceptions to this).

The first source of memes is different from the second source since the meme template in the former is familiar to users outside of Trinidad and Tobago. The second source of internet memes, on the other hand, was drawn from images that are familiar to Trinbagonian users only. Figure 4 is an example of the *Princess Margaret from Debe* meme. This meme is based on a female resident of Debe, an area in south Trinidad, who, in a television news interview, expressed her displeasure with the government's plans to build a highway by accusing the then prime minister of behaving like royalty, 'she feel she is the Princess Margaret' (she thinks she's Princess Margaret), and then proclaiming, 'Me eh fraiding I saying it in big' (I'm not afraid and I'm saying it loudly).

The third category of memes is heavily text-based. However, their memetic quality is achieved due to similarities of form and content. In this third group, the language use of a non-Trinidadian group, often (but not always) identified as American, British, the world, or normal, is highlighted, and the Trinidadian realisation of the same form is juxtaposed directly beneath it. In Figure 5, for example, the Trinidadian pronunciation *mine ears* is pitted against the pronunciation of *mayonnaise* used by the rest of the world.

Although these memes are largely verbal, they sometimes contain national flag emojis or pictures of products. In the meme in Figure 5, for instance, a picture of a Trinidadian brand of mayonnaise, Matouk's, is included. Other memes also contained pictures of the flags of the United States and the United Kingdom. The nature of the memes' content is such that the creators often make use of non-standardised spellings and that two creators may spell the same word differently. Whenever I reproduce memetic content, I will use the spellings used by the creator of the meme to which I am referring.

Figure 5 Mine Ears (Credit: Stinkhtt)

The data set also comprises TikTok videos posted by Kwame Simpson, DeShawn Wiggins, and Stephon Felmine. The three influencers rose to prominence from 2020 onwards through their *Letter of the Day* (*LoD*) videos, originally conceptualised by Simpson but copied by fellow TikTokers Wiggins of Barbados and Felmine of Trinidad and Tobago. In these videos, the vocabulary of the English/Creole of each territory is highlighted and explained to followers in a humorous fashion. In total, the database comprises 126 videos. Each of the videos is quite short, only about 30–45 seconds in length, all collected via TikTok.

The videos were first transcribed orthographically, with the spellings used by the TikToker being preferred over spellings of the local lexical items found in dictionaries. The transcripts were then annotated to highlight Creole features using the markup <Creole></Creole>, with Creole pronunciations further receiving a broad phonetic transcription. An example of this can be seen in (1). In the extract, the verbs *kilketay* and *rush* do not receive a morphological past tense marker, though the use of *was* marks the event as happening the past. In terms of pronunciation, the speaker uses the velarisation of /n/ after LOT vowels in [dɒŋ] and stops the dental fricatives in *the*, producing [di].

(1) <$SF><#>The letter of the day is K <#>K is for kilketay meaning to stumble or fall in a very funny manner <#>For example <#>I [ɐ] was walking along Queen Street and my [mɪ] foot <Creole>gone</Creole> <Creole>down [dɒŋ] </Creole> in a pothole and I <Creole>kilketay</Creole> in front of Jimmy Aboud <#>Or <#>As soon as the dog <Creole>rush</Creole> me [mɪ] I <Creole>kilketay<Creole> in the [di] drain <#>K

In addition to the memes and videos, user interactions also formed part of the data set. A major aspect of the interactive nature of online communication is the possibility to react to posts. On Facebook, this is achieved by clicking on one of six emotional responses – like, love, sad, angry, hug, and wow – while TikTok allows users to love a post by clicking on a heart. The number of reactions to the posts was also recorded.

Beyond interactions, user comments have been frequently used in research on World Englishes in social media, including in studies of the Caribbean. For example, Leung (2017) uses comments from YouTube as a source of attitudinal data, and Mühleisen (2022) uses data from comments in Facebook groups and online forums to study how identity is created. Following these, comments were also included in the present Element. Simpson's TikTok page was hacked, which means that the original comments were lost, so here data is only available for Stephon Felmine and DeShawn Wiggins. The comments were withdrawn manually. For each video, a maximum of twenty-five comments were withdrawn, though several videos contained considerably more comments. This is because a fair proportion of the comments comprised only emojis and did not contain any verbal information. For example, Stephon Felmine's video for the letter U, *uppin*, received 189 comments, but 41 of these are made up solely of strings of the tears of joy emoji or the rolling on the floor laughing emoji. Though these are an important aspect of social media communication, emojis posted without accompanying verbal content will not be analysed here and the comments extracted only comprised those with verbal content.

1.4.2 Ethical Aspects of Social Media Research

The increased interest in language use on social media raises a number of ethical concerns for researchers centred around the notions of ownership of the data and participant consent. The use of social media data in this manner is not unproblematic because it goes against one of the most basic tenets of ethical research: informed consent. Beninger's (2016), study in which she asked social media users for their feelings surrounding the use of social media data for non-social media purposes, obtained mixed results, with users oscillating between two poles: one group who felt informed consent was not needed and another who felt researchers should seek it. The reality, however, is that, given the vast number of social media users, it is almost impossible to track down each user and gain their consent. Memes are generally considered to be in the public domain in social media research (e.g. Chau 2021 and Spilioti 2020 both make use of memes as a source of data) and the memes referred to and reproduced in this Element are all used in accordance with Facebook's fair use policy, which allows for the reproduction of content for education and research purposes.[3] Posts were only taken from groups that were public at the time of data collection, that is, internet users did not have to be a member of the group to access the group's content. The administrators of the Facebook groups were contacted on at least three occasions and Stinkhtt and the Penal Poet granted explicit permission for their memes to be reproduced in this Element. In terms of TikTok videos, the TikTok user agreement informs users of the following:

> You also grant to each user of the Platform a non-exclusive, royalty-free, worldwide licence to access and use your content, including to reproduce (e.g. to copy, share or download), adapt or make derivative works (e.g. to include your content in their content) perform and communicate that content to the public (e.g. to display it) using the features and functions of the Platform for entertainment purposes, subject to your Platform settings.[4]

[3] See 'What Are Fair Use and Other Exceptions to Copyright?' Facebook Help Center (online), www.facebook.com/help/337995452911154.

[4] TikTok, 'Terms of Service' (2023): Section 4.9: 'Ownership of Content and Grant of Licenses', www.tiktok.com/legal/page/eea/terms-of-service/en.

Thus, TikTokers' videos are in the public domain and are freely available for use for other purposes. Nevertheless, I contacted each of the TikTokers to gain their permission to use their content. Only Stephon Felmine responded, and permission was given to reproduce the content.

A second pillar of ethical research is anonymity, and every effort was made to ensure that this could be achieved, particularly in the case of user comments, where informed consent was not possible. Comments were manually extracted from beneath the posts containing memes and videos. Demographic information about the commenters was not stored to protect poster anonymity. The comments were anonymised, and commenter names are not included in this Element. Since the comments are a direct response to the videos and memes, true anonymisation of the data was not possible, since readers are able to go back to the original videos, view them, and read the comments themselves. However, following Durham (2016), the content of the comments was modified slightly and at random so that the propositional content was the same but it would be difficult to match the comment to a specific user retroactively.

Anonymity also means that establishing the authorship of memes can be difficult. Some groups, such as Trinis Be Like, the Penal Poet, and Stinkhtt, include a watermark on the memes they create to establish their provenance, though further demographic information is usually unavailable. It is generally not known whether the administrators of Facebook groups are male or female, Afro- or Indo-Trinidadian, wealthy or working-class, and one cannot be certain whether the content creators live in Trinidad or are part of the Trinbagonian diaspora.[5] Indeed, for some group administrators, anonymity is desirous. When I contacted the administrators of Stinkhtt for permission to use their content and ask for an interview, for example, they replied, 'my current status is that as you may know on the page I try to remain as anonymous as possible so I may not be able to do the zoom interview'.[6]

This lack of demographic information poses a challenge to the analysis of identity since the analyst cannot be completely certain of identity claims relating to relatively fixed demographic factors such as gender, ethnicity, and nationality. Nevertheless, the meme data allows the analyst the chance to look at how aspects of identity are constructed in online spaces. Furthermore, the nature of globalisation and migration adds a further point for consideration in the analysis of the memes. Facebook groups are comprised not only of people resident in Trinidad and Tobago but also of Trinbagonians in the diaspora.

[5] This raises questions as to whether one can be certain that the content creators are Trinbagonian. In short, no. But the claim to Trinidadian identity and the ways in which this is performed can occur independent of place of birth.

[6] Stinkhtt, personal communication, 2023.

Indeed, the ability to connect diasporic and home communities is one attraction of online groups (cf. Honkanen 2020; Mühleisen 2022). Meme creators, likewise, need not be resident in Trinidad and Tobago but, unless the creator identifies their location, the analyst cannot be certain where they are. This raises the question of whether it is productive to examine the memes within a World Englishes framework or whether it may be better to use a translanguaging framework, which is currently more frequently applied in studies of variation in English online and which allows analysts to more readily deal with the varied repertoires that emerge in online communication. However, as I hope my data and analysis will show, such an approach would downplay the very real connections between language, particularly Trinidadian English/Creole, and Trinidadian-ness that the content creators and commenters make.

1.4.3 Data Analysis

The data was analysed using a qualitative discourse analytic approach combined with thematic analyses. The qualitative analysis was done following the principles of multimodal design developed by Kress (2010). For Kress, multimodal design 'refers to the use of different modes – *image*, *writing*, *colour*, *layout* – to present, to realize, at times to (re-)contextualize social positions and relations, as well as *knowledge* in specific *arrangements* for a specific audience' (Kress 2010: 139, italics in original). At the language level, Kress (2010: 79–80) underscores the importance of both lexis and syntax; and in this Element, analysis will focus on the choice of lexical items highlighted both in memes and in TikTok videos as well as the syntactic structures into which the lexical items are embedded, particularly if they are more Creole or standardised English structures. For the videos, attention will be given to the specific pronunciation features used – as captured in the transcription – again focussing on the use of Creole and standardised English forms.

The meme in Figure 6 contains several stereotypical pronunciations of words in Trinidadian English/Creole, represented in eye dialect spelling, though in some cases, such as *x-tray* and *strims*, these spellings have also been recorded in Winer's *Dictionary of the English/Creole of Trinidad and Tobago* (Winer 2009), a major reference work for the variety. The meme contains the pronunciation words *x-ray* [ɛkstre], *shrimps* [strɪmz], *grocery* [goʃri:], *ambulance* [ambrʌlɐns], *picture* [pɪkʧɪə], *bird* [bʌd], and *films* [flɪmz]. Figure 7, in contrast, contains several lexical items that all refer to a person who is easily taken advantage of – *bobolee*, *chupidee*, *dotish*, *cunumunu* (see Winer 2009: 102, 213, 503).

Memes were coded as grammatical if they highlighted an aspect of grammatical variation in Trinidadian English/Creole. The meme in Figure 8 is an

HER: mispronounce dem words again fuh mih nah baby

Figure 6 Mispronounce dem words (Credit: Unknown)

Stranger : What do Trini's mean by "bobolee"
Me: Ah Chupidee
Stranger: What's a Chupidee?
Me: Dotish
Stranger: Dotish?
Me: Ah Cunumunu
@nyc_soca_junkie
Stranger:

Figure 7 Synonyms of stupid (Credit: @nyc_soca_junkie)

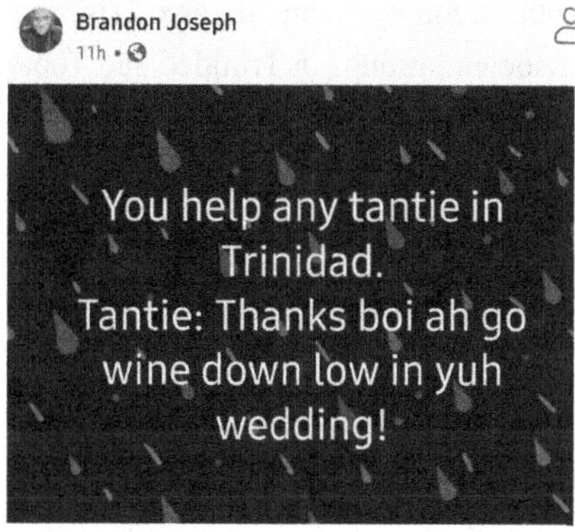

Brandon Joseph
11h
You help any tantie in Trinidad.
Tantie: Thanks boi ah go wine down low in yuh wedding!

Figure 8 Wine down (Credit: Brandon Johnson, Trinis Be Like)

example of a meme that was coded as discourse-pragmatic, since it focusses on the expressions of thanks offered: *ah go wine down at your wedding* is a promise to celebrate all the good things that come to the doer of the good action, as one celebrates at a wedding. It is important to note that an individual meme may contain more than one linguistic feature. Figure 8, for instance, contains the lexical items *tantie* (aunt, or older woman in the community) and *wine* (dance), as well as the grammatical feature *go* future. As such, it can be considered as doing identity work on two levels: highlighting the specific discourse-pragmatic practice and framing this within a general matrix of Trinidadian English/Creole, which further indexes the Trinidadian identity of the speaker.

Once the linguistic foci of the memes were identified, the memes were further analysed to uncover the aspects of identity being performed and the ideologies underlying these performances. This was done using a thematic analysis. An inductive approach was applied, meaning that, instead of using a set of predefined codes, codes were developed based on close analysis of the data.

In a first round of analysis, each meme was studied and coded based on one of two aspects: identity or ideology. Then, a set of criteria based on both linguistic and non-linguistic features was developed. The use of clear criteria ensured that the application of the code was consistent throughout the data, and developing codes for both verbal and non-verbal semiotic aspects meant that the multimodal nature of the memes was considered in the analysis. For identity, four separate codes were developed: Trinbagonian identity, as in Figure 9, in which Trinidadian ailments are presented without reference to ailments in any other variety of English; Trinbagonian identity in relation to American or British English, as in Figure 10, in which the Trinidadian expression for being out on your luck, *crappo smoke yuh pipe*, is juxtaposed to British and American equivalents; Trinbagonian identity in relation to other Caribbean identities, which works in a similar way to the previous group except that the comparison is made to other Caribbean countries; and diverse Trinbagonian identities, that is, in relation to other societal groups in Trinidad and Tobago.

Trinis dont suffer from medical conditions .
We suffer with body parts.

"She does suffer with kidney"
"He does suffer with heart"

Figure 9 Body parts (Credit: @keevontv)

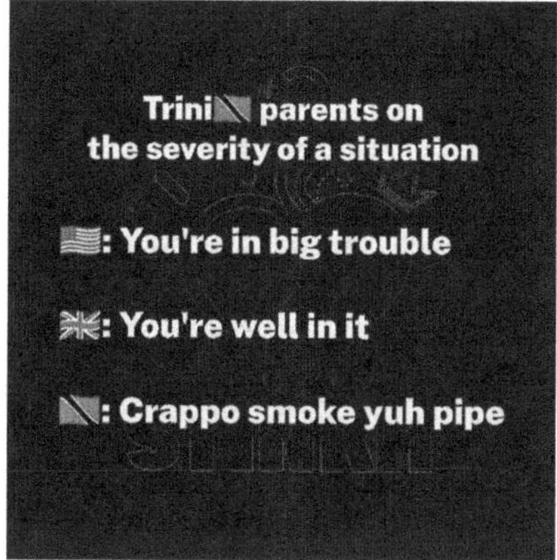

Figure 10 Crappo smoke yuh pipe (Credit: Stinkhtt)

In terms of ideology, there was an overarching standard language ideology that pervaded all the memes and the comments made about them. This was broken down into three main components: Trinidadian English/Creole as funny/humorous, as in (2), where the commenter's contribution is framed by 'haha' and 'LOL' (laughing out loud), suggesting that they find the meme's content to be funny; Trinidadian English/Creole as incorrect or abnormal, as in (3), in which the commenter believes the Trinbagonian word *picker* to be a mispronunciation of another English word and even suggests that such mispronunciations are characteristic of Trinbagonian speech; and Trinidadian English/Creole as a variety on equal footing with metropolitan varieties, such as British or American English, as in (4), where the commenter defends the use of the local pronunciation of *crispy* with metathesis of the /s/ and /p/ sounds, resulting in [krɪpsi:] .

(2) haha i remember this. No i never did but i have older sisters who did lol.

(3) probably a mispronunciation (as usual) of pricker, meaning a prickle or thorn

(4) But it is cripsy! Everyone else wrong

Table 1 contains an overview of the codes used for the memes data and the criteria for identity and ideological markers in the memes.

Kress's (2010: 154) approach to multimodality also stresses the importance of layout in terms of dircction of the text, how it is centred, and whether it is presented in a vertical or horizontal manner, and this will also be considered here in the analysis of the memes. This is also important for understanding the videos, since they often have text embedded into them as, for example, headlines. Beyond text, a multimodal analysis accounts for the use of both images

Table 1 Overview of coding system of memes and comments

General code	Specific sub-code	Linguistic identifiers	Non-linguistic criteria
Identity			
	Trinbagonian identity	Mention of Trinidad or Tobago without opposing element	Use of Trinidad and Tobago flag, national colours, or cultural emblems
	Trinbagonian vs American or British	Identification of specific country	Use of flag emojis Use of colour
	Trinidadian versus other Caribbean	Identification of specific territory, notably Guyana	Use of flag emojis Use of colour
	Different groups of Trinidadians	Naming of a specific group, e.g. 'Hindu girls who went Convent'	None observed
Ideologies	Trinidadian English/Creole as funny		Laughing emoji within the layout of the meme or the caption
	Trinidadian English/Creole as incorrect/ abnormal	Words such as 'normal' or 'regular' presented in apposition with Trinidadian English/Creole feature Words that treat Trinidadian English/Creole as incorrect, e.g. 'mispronounce'	Tick mark or X symbols signifying right or wrong. Positioning of Trinidadian variant below other variant
	Trinidadian English/Creole as correct or equal to metropolitan variety		Positioning of Trinidad English/ Creole variant adjacent to metropolitan variety

and colour (Kress 2010: 159). Images are a central aspect of image macro memes, since meaning-making in this regard is tied to the reproduction of the meme and how it is recontextualised and given additional meanings by new users. Other aspects within the memes include the use of emojis, which are especially important because they give critical emotional information (Jovanovic and Van Leeuwen 2018). The use of colour is also crucial here, since content creators of both memes and videos can draw on colour as an 'ideational resource' (Kress, 2010: 59). The visual is, of course, a core element of video productions. For the videos, the analysis considered elements of costuming, properties, and other background images that were included in the video, such as the use of flags or pictures of specific places or people.

2 Identities and Ideologies in Facebook Memes

2.1 Introduction

This section considers how identity is performed in memes, the ideologies underlying these identity claims and looks at how memes contribute to the (re-)production and circulation of language ideologies. The multimodal nature of the memes is unpacked using a semiotic analysis and by drawing on recent sociological work on Trinidadian culture.

2.2 Language and Identity in Memes

2.2.1 Trinidadian Identity on Its Own

Trinidadian meme creators make use of all levels of the linguistic system in constructing diverse aspects of Caribbean identity and, more specifically, a Trinidadian identity within a larger Caribbean identity. This is mostly signalled at the discourse/pragmatic level – claiming practices that set Caribbean forms of communication apart from similar practices in other countries. Such memes build on the (real or imagined) notion of a shared Caribbean identity, realised linguistically through Caribbean standardised English or common features across Caribbean Creoles. In Figure 11, Caribbean parents' methods of motivating their children to speak with confidence are highlighted in the expression *asking meh or telling meh* (are you sure/certain), a question that arises because the speaker's tone and intonation suggest insecurity. Here, an aspect of culture (child-rearing) is linked to specific linguistic practices.

This identity is not claimed solely by the content creator. Several commenters express agreement with the meme's content, often seeing themselves or others in the meme. In (5), for instance, the commenter admits to using the expression *asking or telling* with their sons, claiming the identity of Caribbean parent for themself.

Figure 11 Asking or telling (Credit: @keevotv)

(5) [2 emojis] I am Caribbean parent . . . .. yuh asking meh . . . or yuh telling meh . . . which one???? to my sons [emoji] [3 rolling on the floor laughing emojis][7]

In (6), the commenter associates the expression with his father, creating a link between a person known to be a Caribbean parent and the expression. In this way, commenters contribute to the enregisterment of the language, by associating the language with 'characterlogical figures and personae' and connecting this language with 'social types of persons, real or imagined, whose voices they take them to be' (Agha 2005: 38).

(6) I swear full on hear my father full tone with this yes! the trauma of second guessing if the answer or assume if the man being rhetorical!! Hahahaha

Indeed, the comments suggest a strong Trinidadian affiliation with the content, even though the meme clearly states, 'Caribbean people'. The meme garners 132 comments, eight of which refer to a particular place or nationality. Of these eight, two refer to Caribbean or West Indies people (7), one refers to Trinbago people (8), one to Trinidad and Trinidadians (9) and the last refers to a specific place in Trinidad (Beetham Market, (10)). Particularly noteworthy in (8) and (9) is the use of pronouns. In (8), the poster claims ownership of the community with the use of *my*, while in (9) the poster highlights their membership in the community through the use of *we*.

(7) Always Bad News! Funny West Indies People.

(8) My TRINIBAGO People Not Easy

(9) If it's so we just say it. Trini say plain talk bad manners. Trini ain't have manners at all at all at all [shocked emoji, Trinidad and Tobago emojis, three rolling on the floor laughing emojis]

(10) Yes. But dem ladies who sell Bush at the Beetham Market helped my son with he Bush Medicine

[7] Some emojis could not be reproduced in print. These have been replaced by verbal descriptions of the relevant emojis in their location in the original online text.

The non-linguistic aspects of the memes suggest that the Trinidadian identity is still subsumed within the Caribbean identity. This is achieved through the use of colour. Keevan, the influencer in Figure 11, is clad in a red suit with a red tie, possibly because, based on the background of his picture, the photo was taken around Christmas but also signalling the main colour of the national flag of Trinidad and Tobago. Of course, several other Caribbean countries have red in their national flags (Antigua and Barbuda, Grenada, Dominica, St Kitts and Nevis), but Keevan's red clothing, coupled with his Trinidadian heritage, arguably does more to index Trinidad and Tobago than pan-Caribbean-ness.

2.2.2 Trinidadian English/Creole versus British or American English as Part of Identity

Most often, however, Trinidadian identity in memes is created in relation to other groups, named and unnamed. In this regard, Trinidadian English/Creole and its users are presented as unique – a people set apart from all other speakers of English. This is especially true in the 'Trinidad versus the world' series memes in which features of language that are felt to be peculiar to Trinidad are highlighted and presented as being so special that they cannot be heard anywhere else in the world. In Figure 12, aspects of pronunciation of the word *broth* are compared: [brɒθ] for the world versus [brɒf] in Trinidad. Figure 13 compares the vocabulary item *tush* meaning *turn*.

The Trinidadian-ness of the terms is highlighted via the use of emojis of the Trinidad and Tobago flag that accompany the word 'Trinidad' in both Figures 12 and 13. This form of Trinidadian exceptionalism, that is, the belief that Trinidad stands apart from all other countries, has been observed elsewhere (on Trinidad carnival culture, cf. Wainwright 2022).

Figure 12 Broff (Credit: Trinis Be Like)

Figure 13 Tush (Credit: Trinis Be Like)

Furthermore, the identification with extraordinariness is echoed in users' comments throughout the data set, as seen in (11)–(14). Linguistic identity in this regard is sometimes linked to feelings of national pride (11) but can also be linked to more derisive views, such as instability (12). Commenters' contributions reinforce a shared identity grounded in the notion of collective distinction where Trinidad is a special place (12), Trinidadians are special people (13), and Trinidadian English/Creole is a special language (14).

(11) Unapologetically [Trinidad and Tobago emoji]

(12) Only in Trinidad where half the country mad

(13) No people like Trinis

(14) Trinbagonian is a very colorful language! There are so many ways to tell someone that they are stupid!

In addition to generic comparisons, identity in memes is also created by contrasting Trinidadian English/Creole with named varieties. Frequently, Trinidadian English/Creole is presented in contrast with British or American English. Examples of this can be seen in Figures 14 and 15.

In Figure 14, the onomatopoeic *kootooks*, the sound made by a head being hit, is contrasted with *knocked/hit in the head*. In Figure 15, the Trinidadian expression for unpleasant body odour, *smell ripe*, is highlighted. In each meme, Trinidadian English/Creole is placed in contrast to British and/or American English, and the content creators seem to define Trinidadian English/Creole in terms of these varieties. By extension, linguistic identity could be argued to be established in relation to and defined as a rejection of metropolitan varieties, since the Trinidadian word is presented as an alternative to these. Visually, this is established through the use of images of national flags.

Figure 14 Kootooks (Credit: @Trinibakkhanal)

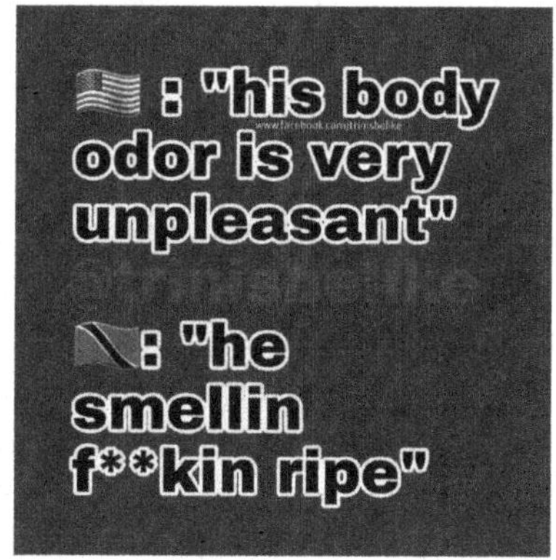

Figure 15 Ripe (Credit: Trinis Be Like)

However, flags or verbal identification of the varieties are not always necessary. In memes using the *Woman Yelling at Cat* template (Figure 16), there is no overt mention of any variety and no obvious semiotic clues about the varieties of English being compared. Instead, content creators rely on context and shared knowledge to convey their meanings. In Figure 16, the content creators rely on the receivers' knowledge of how the meme works – that the woman is wrong and the cat is right. Secondly, the meme creators depend on receivers' familiarity with the scheme of juxtaposing Trinidadian English/Creole against British or American English present in other meme schema. Since the memes appear in Trinidadian-identifying Facebook groups, this helps with this possible interpretation. Finally, the content creators assume that the receivers are familiar with the term *birth paper* (a document recording a person's birth), and the pronunciation [bɜːd pepə], as stereotypical Trinidadian pronunciation of this

Figure 16 Bird paper (Credit: Nashoon Alexander)

lexical item, and so will be able to conclude that the cat's response represents Trinidadian English/Creole.

The pitting of Trinidadian norms against British and American norms in memes is not surprising; other research has examined multinormativity in Caribbean Englishes and Trinidadian English in contexts such as newspaper writing (Hackert and Deuber 2015) and education (Meer et al. 2019; Hänsel and Meer 2023), and has found evidence of changing phonological orientations (Deuber and Leung 2013; Meer et al. 2019), grammatical uses, and lexical orientations (G. Wilson 2023), so the folk linguistic concerns observed here align with these. However, where scholarly research has consistently reported distancing away from Creole, the overt identification with Creole forms in the comments suggest that this need not always be the case.

2.2.3 Trinidadian Identity versus Other Caribbean Identities

Trinidadian identity was also highlighted in contrast to other Caribbean identities, particularly Guyanese. Guyanese English/Creole became the target of Trinidadian ridicule in late 2020, when an online feud emerged over the correct word order of the phrase *curry chicken* (Trinidad) or *chicken curry* (Guyana). Interest in the topic was widespread, and it therefore became the subject of several memes. The Trinidadian content creators generated a number of memes in which Guyanese English/Creole is vilified. Indeed, the feud went on for such a long time that the Guyanese president, Dr Mohamed Irfaan Ali, referred to it in a speech at the Caribbean Agri Expo in August 2022, when, in a conciliatory effort, he said, 'my friends in Trinidad and Tobago, whether it's curry chicken or chicken curry, we will have curry'. President Ali's attempt towards unity across

When a #Trini hears a #guyanese
person say chicken curry.

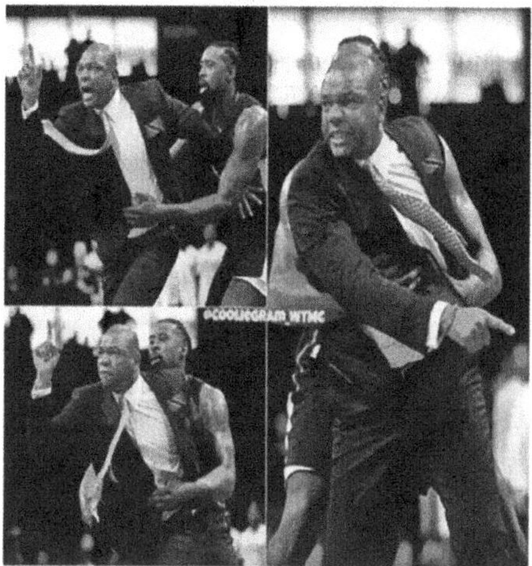

Figure 17 Angry over curry (Credit: Unknown)

the two nations contradicts the quite separate identities that the memes underscore. The Guyanese *chicken curry* is presented as ridiculous and a source of anger (Figure 17).

In this meme, the hearer's ears have been so offended by *chicken curry* that he must be physically restrained. In other memes, aspects of popular culture are used to underscore the notion of Guyanese English/Creole being ridiculous by extrapolating that the fast-food chain KFC (Kentucky Fried Chicken) would be different in Guyana (Kentucky Chicken Fried, Figure 18). Guyanese English/Creole is thus presented as ridiculous in comparison to Trinidadian English/Creole, and Trinidadian online identity is linked to the perceived superiority of that variety.

The *chicken curry/curry chicken* debate highlights the importance of stereotypes in creating linguistic identities. There are a number of systematic differences between Guyanese and Trinidadian English Creoles, but these are almost never drawn on in the memes. Indeed, during the entire data collection period, I came across only one meme that highlights another difference between the two varieties, the *Starbax Caffee* meme on the Penal Poet's page. This meme draws on phonetic differences in the realisation of the STRUT lexical set in Trinidadian and Guyanese English/Creole, realised as [ʌ] in Trinidadian but [a] in Guyanese. Even though it obtains 338 likes and 108 comments and is shared 862 times, other meme creators do not draw on this feature in making further memes.

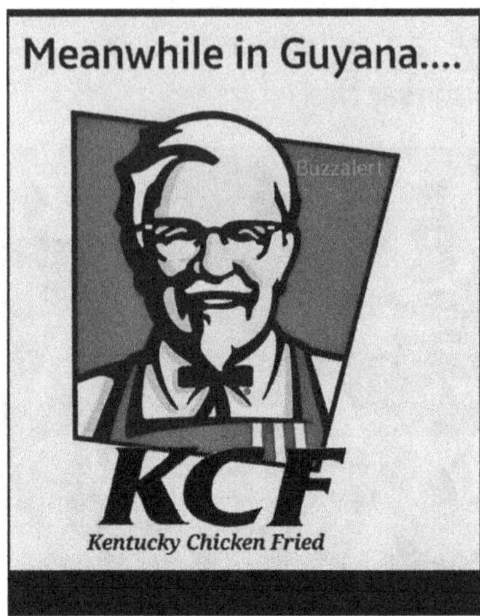

Figure 18 Kentucky Chicken Fried (Credit: Unknown)

The memes about Guyanese English/Creole are, on the surface, presented in the spirit of fun. However, there are more cynical and even xenophobic undertones that arise in the memes. The meme in Figure 19 plays with the stereotype of reverse word order in Guyanese English/Creole by extending it to individual words, here switching the order of the syllables in *gramoxone*, a powerful pesticide used in gardening. The use of rolling on the floor laughing emojis in the background highlights the fact that the creator intends their contribution to be taken as a joke. But the meme teeters between the comic and the caustic: Guyana is known to have one of the highest suicide rates in the world, and the most common cause of death by suicide is consumption of pesticides such as gramoxone (Shaw et al. 2022).

The deluge of *curry chicken/chicken curry* memes is not amusing to all members of the Facebook groups in which they appear. Figure 19 receives few reactions, and commenters point out that the meme maker has gone too far. Extract (15) is taken from an exchange between two users of the Stinkhtt Facebook page. Commenter A argues that other Trinidadians should abandon the meme on the grounds that the celebrity chef Gordon Ramsay and Indians from India also use the Guyanese word order, and calls the linguistic wordplay xenophobic. Author B, however, insists that it is meant as fun, labelling it 'inter-regional picong' (teasing). Author B's use of the word *picong* further aligns them with the Trinidadian speech community and highlights their Trinidadian identity.

Figure 19 Xone-gramo (Credit: unknown)

(15) A: Gordon frickin Ramsay says chicken curry and vegetable curry, Indians from India say chicken curry, can we just let it go.
B: Nah it's fun.
A: Yes xenophobia is a joke, I forgot that.
B: Ain't no fear of Guyanese. They're normal people. It's just inter-regional picong.
A: Uh huh. From a country whose people complain that Guyanese were taking their jobs, and now it's Venezuelans. No thanks.

As Kerrigan explains:

> [p]icong in Trinidad is usually a safe way to poke at perceived differences in race and ethnicity ... Mostly, picong is used by many Trinbagonians to heckle and mock each other's differences and similarities in a friendly manner and poke fun at persons or issues in popular culture or around politics ... The line between humor and insult in picong is fine and constantly shifting. However, the convivial spirit of picong rarely degenerates into heated debates or physical altercations. (Kerrigan 2016: 743)

However, in this instance, the performance of picong is not completely successful and the line between 'humor and insult' seems to have been crossed.

Commenter A in (15) notes that Venezuelan immigrants in Trinidad are also subject to discrimination, which becomes apparent in language-related memes. Following the economic crisis and civil unrest in Venezuela since 2015, there has been relatively large-scale migration from Venezuela to Trinidad, separated from each other by only seven miles. The vulnerable Venezuelans have not received the support they might have hoped for, as documented in a report by the United Nations High Commission for Refugees (UNHCR) in 2018, and are often victims of xenophobia.

Where in the case of Guyana the focus of memes was Guyanese English/ Creole, the memes that highlight Venezuelan immigrants focus on their Spanish in contrast to English (Figures 20 and 21). Both memes contain the derogatory reference to Venezuelans, *Venes* or *Venis*. Figure 20 is first and foremost a reference to how *maxi taxis*, privately owned buses integral to the public transportation system, are loaded. 'One to go' is the call maxi drivers and conductors use to attract passengers to their buses (regardless of how many seats are actually empty). In the meme, *andale* (come on) replaces 'one to go' and suggests that a Venezuelan maxi driver or conductor is not a competent speaker of English. Moreover, the expression 'andale andale Arima Arima' is a play on the words 'andale andale, arriba arriba', the catchphrase of the cartoon mouse Speedy Gonzales, a popular character known for his oversized sombrero, his red neckerchief, and his exaggerated Mexican English accent, and the subject of much discussion about racist stereotypes in media and popular culture (Behnken and Smithers 2015). The replacement of Speedy Gonzales's 'arriba' (English: above) with a rhyming Trinidadian place name, Arima, a major transport hub, links Venezuelans to this stereotype and serves to separate them linguistically from the English/ Creole-speaking Trinidadian community.

The idea of Venezuelan immigrants as not having mastered English also appears in comments under memes, even memes that do not refer to Venezuelans. For example, in (17), a comment found under a meme about Guyanese English/Creole, a commenter notes that the word order of *chicken curry/curry chicken* is of no consequence since someone purchasing this would be given the right product regardless of the request, a fact to which even Spanish speakers can attest. The use of the form *speaky* further highlights the xenophobic tone in this meme.

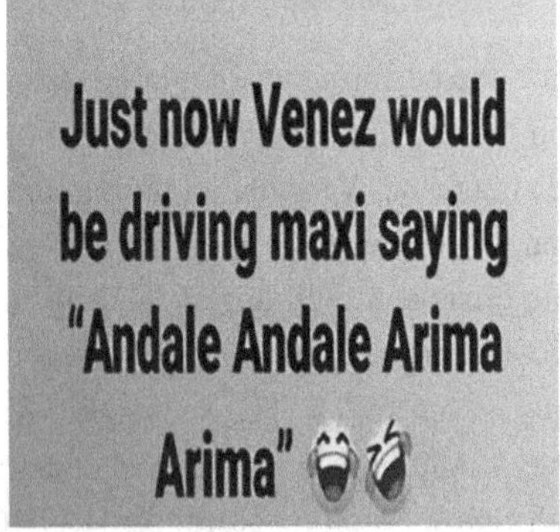

Figure 20 Andale Arima (Credit: Stinkhtt)

Figure 21 Parang (Credit: *Stinkhtt*)

(16) Makes no difference cause you'll get exactly what you want. Ask those who no speaky ingles.

The notion of the linguistic separation between Spanish-speaking Venezuelans and English/Creole Trinidadians is also seen in Figure 21. Here, however, it is the Trinidadians whose language is deficient. Parang is a traditional Trinidadian musical form sung around Christmas time. It has strong links to Venezuela and is typically sung in Spanish, though contemporary parang contains more English (Brown 2009: 22). However, as Brown (2009) notes, few people in Trinidad speak and understand Spanish. This lack of competence no doubt produces performances that, according to the creator of the meme in Figure 21, do not make sense to Venezuelan listeners ('singing shit'). Thus, Trinidadian identity in this regard is presented as an inability to speak or sing in Spanish accurately.

2.2.4 Different Groups of Trinidadians

The final way in which the language in memes is used to create identities concerns the creation of separate identities within the Trinidadian society. In this regard, three distinct groups are singled out: South Trinidadians, Convent Girls, and Bakayard Trinis. Geographical and social stereotypes in Trinidad are often ways of encoding racial and socioeconomic tensions and stereotypes. For example, understandings of north and south have their antecedents in the early post-emancipation and indentureship period, in which the newly freed Africans left the plantations and tended to settle in the area surrounding the capital Port-of-Spain (the north), while East Indian indentured labourers were often paid with a parcel of land in villages such as Fyzabad and Barrackpore in south Trinidad (Ehrlich 1971). Bakayard Trinis is less obviously racially charged. The large working-class African post-emancipation population often found housing in barrack yards and tenements (Brereton 2010). The phonological similarities between *barrack yard* and *bakayard* are almost too obvious to highlight and, though etymologically no link between the two forms has been documented, there is an adjectival meaning of barrack yard which means 'loud, vulgar or uneducated' (Winer 2009: 56). The term 'Convent Girls' initially referred to girls educated at St Joseph's Convent, Port-of-Spain. The school was opened in 1836 for the education of planters' daughters and had a majority white population until the 1960s, when Independence meant the school was open to all. Nevertheless, it is still dominated by girls from middle- and upper-middle-class sectors of the society. More recently, the term has been used to describe any girl attending an all-girls' school in Trinidad, such as Naparima Girls' College, Holy Name Convent, or Bishop Anstey High School.

Perceptions of linguistic distinction between Trinidadians from the north and south of the country have been documented in previous sociolinguistic work on the island (Stell 2018). Among the features that Stell's respondents list as evidence of regional variation in Trinidad is the compound pronoun *my one*, associated with South Trinidadian speech (Stell 2018: 128), and this association is also seen by the poster of Figure 22. As in the memes that separated Trinidadian English/Creole from other varieties, the meme in Figure 22 makes the claim that the language of residents of South Trinidad is somehow anomalous, that is, different from 'everyone else's' speech. Here, too, the order of the elements is important. In placing the way 'everyone else' speaks first, above the speech of 'South people', the two varieties are placed in a hierarchical relationship, with everyone else's language at the top.

The responses to this meme, however, show that linguistic identities are rather more complex than the poster imagines. Few commenters agree with the meme, acknowledging that the compound pronoun is a 'south thing' (17).

(17) See it's a south thing

However, the overall reaction to this meme is quite negative. The meme generates a number of comments rejecting the claim, as seen in extracts (18)–(21). In (18), the poster claims affiliation with South Trinidad ('I'm from South') but outright rejects 'my one' as a feature of their speech. Other commenters, such as those in (19) and (20), dismiss the meme as erroneous, a 'damn lie' invented by a 'delusional' individual.

(18) I'm from South and I say neither eh

(19) Damn lie!

Everyone else : My own
South Trinidad : My one

Figure 22 My one

(20) Exactly. I never really heard nobody from South talk so first to begin with So this poster is just delusional SMH

Still other posters correct the geographical provenance of form, Central Trinidad (21).

(21) Mostly central Trinidad

The desire to distance themselves from the feature seems, in some ways, to work counter to the general trend in the data for features of Trinidadian English/Creole to awaken feelings of pride in the online community. However, it certainly does not seem to be the case that commenters do not wish to identify with Trinidadian English/Creole at all, and several of their posts contain Trinidadian English/Creole features, such as the discourse marker *eh* (18) and the use of *does* to signal habitual action (22). Instead, it seems that *my one* is highly stigmatised; the feature appears on the list of features listed as examples of Bad English in Winford's study of language attitudes among trainee teachers (Winford 1976: 52).

(22) South ppl doesn't say that . . . 'certain people' say that.

Moreover, some of these reactions seem to be racially motivated. While the Facebook groups used for data in this Element do not contain overt instances of hate speech and particularly racist language, such platforms do exist on social media, reflecting the tensions between the two largest ethnic groups in the country: Afro- and Indo-Trinidadians. Central Trinidad and South Trinidad are, historically, the regions with the larger Indo-Trinidadian populations. So, when the commentor in (20) says, 'certain people' say *my one*, and not 'South people', they seem to be drawing a distinction between Afro-Trinidadians and Indo-Trinidadians resident in South Trinidad and attributing the feature to the latter group.Similarly, the association in (21) of *my one* with Central Trinidad also places the feature on the lips of the Indo-Trinidadian community there.

A second group whose language comes under scrutiny in the memes is Convent and Naps Girls, treated in this analysis as Convent Girls. The 'convent accent' phenomenon has been documented in several recent studies on Trinidadian English/Creole (see Ferreira and Heitmeier 2015; Deuber, Hänsel, and Westphal 2021; Meer and Fuchs 2022) and is strongly associated with standardised Trinidadian English (Deuber et al. 2021: 449). Though the accent is yet to be fully described, it is clear that Convent Girls are stereotyped as a distinct speech community within the larger Trinidadian community. Meme makers view the use of Trinidadian English/Creole as an essential aspect of

Trinidadian identity. Accordingly, Convent and Naps Girls are stripped of this identity since they are perceived as sounding different, so different in fact that they are no longer part of that community, their speech being likened to American accents. Therefore, they are wished a 'happy 4th of July' (Figure 23), assumed to be celebrating US Independence and not that of Trinidad and Tobago on 31 August; they are, after all, 'American citizens' (Figure 24).

Meme creators also use Convent and Naps Girls' speech to isolate them from other groups of Trinidadians and communities of which they may be part. Thus, the maker of the meme in Figure 25 denies Hindu Convent Girls linguistic affiliation with their religious community, asserting that they would call *roat* (sweet flour-based confection shared at Divali) 'Hanuman cookies'.

Figure 23 Happy Independence (Credit: Unknown)

Figure 24 American citizens (Credit: Unknown)

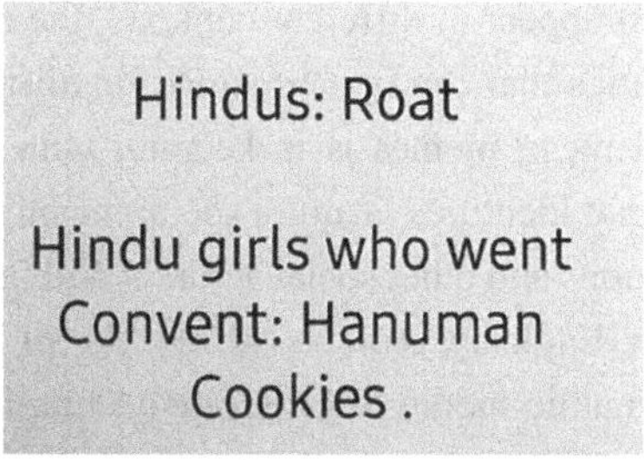

Hindus: Roat

Hindu girls who went Convent: Hanuman Cookies .

Figure 25 Hanuman cookies (Credit: Trinis Be Like)

Figure 26 Investiquire (Credit: Trinis Be Like)

Convent Girls' speech is also placed in opposition to the speech of 'Bakayad' Trinis, that is, Trinidadians who are considered to be down to earth (Figure 26). There are racist undertones here, too, with historically white Convent Girls having their language pitted against that of the Black and Brown residents of the barrack yard. In both Figures 25 and 26, the Convent Girls' language is marked by American lexis ('cookies') and idiomatic expressions ('check it out'). In the latter case, Convent speech is also marked as conforming to external standardised English grammatical norms ('Let's'), rather than Trinidadian English/ Creole grammar ('lewwe' [let+ we]). This is in keeping with presentation of Convent Girls as American citizens. Their language use is presented in such a way that they become inauthentic Trinidadians, where authenticity seems to be linked to more grassroots identities.

In identifying distinct groups of Trinidadians and separating them on the basis of their language, the meme makers assert their own Trinidadian identity in relation to these groups. And because the memes are not all produced by the same people, or at least appear in different contexts, the memes point towards a multiplicity of identities that can be performed linguistically. The relational nature of identity-making in memes is in keeping with Bucholtz and Hall's (2005: 598) assertion that identities 'acquire social meaning in relation to other available identity positions and other social actors'. Within the World Englishes paradigm, Trinidadian English/Creole is firmly set in the fourth phase of Schneider's (2007) dynamic model of postcolonial Englishes: endonormative stabilisation. In terms of identity work, this phase is characterised by the local variety of English being used as a symbol of a shared local identity, defined in part through the relationship with external norms. The memes that highlight shared Trinidadian identity, pitting Trinidadian English against 'the world' or else specifically against British or American English, no doubt achieve this.

At the same time, the meme makers' nuanced understanding of linguistic variation in Trinidad suggests that, developmentally, Trinidadian English/Creole might have entered the final phase of differentiation, at least in some respects. At this stage, there is variation across groups within the nation, whereby 'individuals therefore align and define themselves as members of smaller, sociolinguistically determined groups: as people of a certain gender, age or ethnicity; through living in a certain area or locality; as members of a certain social group or stratum, and they derive primary as well as hybrid identities from these group membership patterns' (Schneider 2007: 53). While there have been studies that examine internal variation in Trinidadian English/Creole, these have often focussed on macro-sociolinguistic factors, most notably ethnicity (Leung and Deuber 2014; Gooden and Drayton 2017) and urban versus rural locality (Winford 1978; Leung 2013). These large-scale categories also arise in the memes data, as in references to South people, Sangre Grande, and central. Yet the memes data suggests that there is a range of micro-social factors that are relevant to identity-making both in the physical space of Trinidad and in the online Trinidianosphere.

2.3 Language Ideologies in Memes

Underlying these performances of identity in memes is an overarching standard language ideology. This standard language ideology is manifested in several, interrelated ways in the memes and the comments: one which sees external norms/standards, particularly British or American norms, as correct; one which sees Trinidadian English/Creole as corrupt; one which sees Trinidadian English/Creole as the norm. The first of these ideologies is manifested most clearly in references to standard English as correct. Specifically, Standard British English is held in high regard, and British norms are used as the main point of comparison.

This can be seen in (23), where the commenter argues that the British pronunciation of 'medicine' is the 'correct way'.

(23) This is actually how the British pronounce it. So seeing as it's their language I assume that's the correct way. Could be wrong though

Trinidadian English/Creole, on the other hand, is something that cannot be comprehended by speakers of standardised varieties such as American English (24).

(24) These Americans won't understand

In the *curry chicken/chicken curry* debate, two commenters, in extracts (16) and (25), make direct reference to British norms. In (16), the reference is to the British celebrity chef Gordon Ramsay's use of 'chicken curry' and in (25) the poster argues that 'British friends' are among those that can correct them. Furthermore, both the commenters in (16) and (25) make a reference to other external groups 'Indians from India' (16) and 'Indian and South East Asian' friends (25). This appeal to ethnic Indians outside of Trinidad or Guyana is also ideological. It undermines the authority and claims to authenticity of Indo-Trinidadians by forcing their linguistic glance outwards.

(25) To be fair though I'm guessing most of the world says chicken curry and not curry chicken but my Indian, South East Asian and British friends can correct me

The corollary of this ideology is that Trinidadian English/Creole is viewed as inferior to metropolitan varieties. This is unwittingly achieved through the layout of the memes, in which the text appears with the British or American variants in first place, either at the top or on the left, and the Trinidadian English/Creole variant at the bottom or on the right. Van Leeuwen and Kress (1995: 28) argue that '[w]hen a layout polarizes top and bottom, placing different, perhaps contrasting, elements in the upper and lower sections of the page, the elements placed on top are presented as the Ideal and those placed at the bottom as the Real'. The same holds for left to right ordering for information structuring, in which given information appears first (on the left) and new information appears afterwards. Van Leeuwen and Kress state that the new information 'is therefore in principle problematic, contestable, the information at issue, while the Given is presented as commonsense and selfevident' (Van Leeuwen and Kress 1995: 27). These layouts are used consistently in the *World versus Trinidad* trope, as well as in the *Woman Yelling at Cat* meme. Thus, in Figures 12–16, the World, British, and American variants are presented as the ideal, whereas the Trinidadian variant is less glamourous. Similarly, in the *Woman Yelling at Cat* meme, British and American variants are 'commonsense and selfevident' whereas the Trinidadian variants become in some ways 'problematic' or contestable. In many ways, the hierarchical ordering of varieties in these memes very closely resembles the hierarchy presented in Mair's (2013) world system of Englishes model, where the 'hypercentral' American English is listed at the top, followed by 'supercentral' British English, and then 'central' (peripheral?) Trinidadian English/Creole.

The possible peripherality of Trinidadian English/Creole is further underscored by its inferior status, even among its own speakers. The meme in Figure 27 reproduces the belief that Trinidadian English/Creole is in some ways broken or not fit for purpose, like the car in the bottom frame, compared with standardised English, the target variety. Interestingly enough, although this meme is circulated in Trinidadian-identifying Facebook groups, the *English in my mind/English I speak* trope with the car imagery is common on social media and I was able to find the same or similar memes on several platforms: Facebook (e.g. Muthal Memes, a page sharing memes on Indian culture); Twitter (@TheScoreBooster, the Twitter handle of an online test prep company that offers IELTS coaching); LinkedIn (e.g. Career For All, a job-posting site based in Dubai, Kuwait, and Pakistan); and YouTube (e.g. Daily Juicy Memes 365). The presence of this meme on the Trinidadian-identifying website suggests that

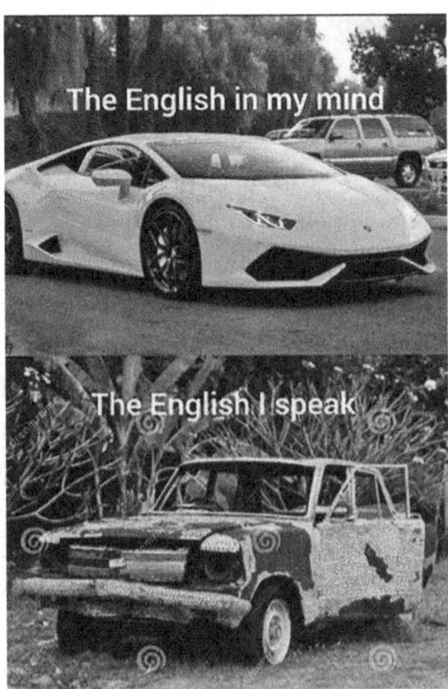

Figure 27 English in my mind

concerns surrounding rightness and wrongness are not unique to Trinidadian users and that this aspect of the standard language ideology is global and is circulated via globalisation's major tool: the internet. What does appear to be different, however, is the ludic tone of these memes, which belies the offline repercussions of speaking 'the English I speak', since humour is particularly resonant in Trinidadian memes.

The supposed inferior status of Trinidadian English/Creole is also reflected in users' comments. The use of Trinidadian English/Creole is linked to poor education – indeed illiteracy – by the poster in (26), who rejects a previous commentor's claim that the use of the *does* habitual is acceptable across the Caribbean.

(26) No it's not acceptable, It's acceptable for ILLITERATE Caribbean people and you're implying ALL Caribbean people are illiterate

For other commenters, Trinidadian English/Creole is viewed as an under-developed form of English – its speakers 'barely speak English' – at best comparable with baby talk, 'twinidadyan' (27). Trinidadian English/Creole is a language of insane people (28), living in an imaginary land (29), or 'a wrongside kinda place' (30). Like the dilapidated car in Figure 27, the commenter in (31) also sees Trinidadian English/Creole as broken, chopped up 'like roast pork', and ruined by covering it with ketchup, referring to the Trinidadian practice of adding ketchup to all meals as a form of gravy and food colouring (M. Wilson 2023).

(27) Some of us Trinis barely speak English. We speak twinidadyan

(28) Only in Trinidad where half the country mad

(29) Only in the imaginary land of Trinidad

(30) Trinidad is a wrongside kinda place. Trini does take the English language interpret it how they feel chop it up like roast pork and pour ketchup all over it

Comments such as these seem counter to two decades of research that has consistently reported improving attitudes towards Trinidadian English/Creole (e.g. Mühleisen 2001). They are perhaps best taken as evidence for the existence of a culture of gatekeeping on social media, which may not be reflective of language ideologies on the whole. Indeed, most of the reactions to the memes on social media are quite positive, and most of the comments suggest a sense of solidarity with and pride in Trinidadian English/Creole.

Above all, the memes and reactions to them highlight an ideology that links Trinidadian English/Creole to humour and laughter. This is seen through the use of laughing emojis within the emoji content but also through the distribution of the reactions to the memes. Facebook allows users on its platform to respond to posts non-verbally by selecting a reaction based on one of seven toggles: like, love, care, LOL, wow, sad, and angry. Using a subsample of the data (n = 40 memes), the distribution of reactions was recorded. In total, Facebook users reacted to the forty memes 9,659 times, with the vast majority of these being LOLs, which accounted for 66 per cent of all reactions (6,321 reactions). The next most popular reaction, like, had slightly less than half the total as LOL, accounting for 32 per cent of the total and 3,097 reactions. The overall distribution of reactions is shown in Figure 28.

The comments beneath the memes also confirm the convivial nature of the memes. This is seen in direct comments which state that the commenter finds something funny (31); in the use of netspeak abbreviations such as LMAO (laughing my ass off) (32), which may include further commentary; or commenters displaying their own verbal dexterity by building on the joke in the meme.

(31) That's hilarious

(32) LMFAO I read this in your voice

The exchange in (33) is taken from the comments below Figure 29, the *Trinidad on the Moon* meme. This is one of the most popular memes in the corpus, with more than 1,038 reactions, most of which, 743, are LOL, suggesting that the majority of people who reacted to the meme found it funny. The

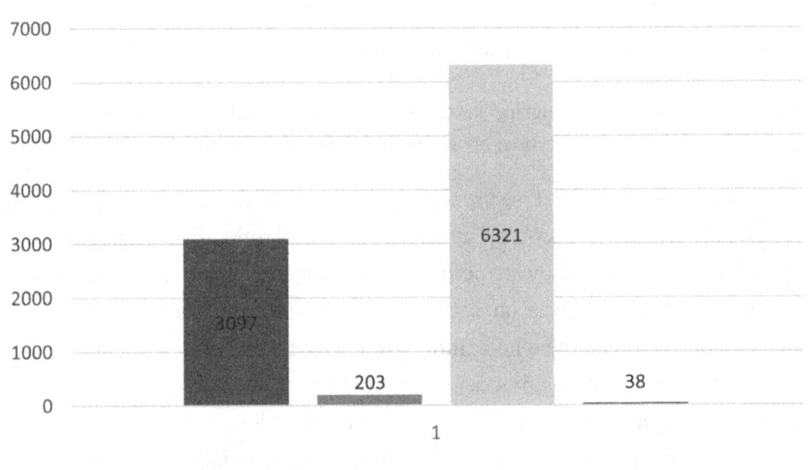

Figure 28 Reactions to Facebook memes

WHEN AMERICA GOES ON THE MOON
"That's one small step for man, one giant leap for mankind."
IF TRINIDAD GOES ON THE MOON...
Yes all yuh. We on the mooooonnnn. I want to big up everybody watching right now. Mummy and dem in Sando. Oh gorm, we seeing Trinidad from up here. Big up!

Figure 29 Trinidad on the moon

meme pokes fun at the Trinidadian practice of bigging up on radio call-in shows, whereby callers greet the radio host and proceed to greet friends and family members (see Mühleisen 2022: 133–158). The parodic elements of the meme are taken up by commenters A and B, who jointly create a setting in which lunar life takes on darker aspects of Trinidadian life: poorly maintained roads and infrastructure, criminality marked by the cultivation of marijuana, murder, and the presence of gangs. The element of humour is retained through the mention of the 'allyuh too wicked' trope. The expression has come to be associated with the mothers of violent criminals in lower socio-economic communities who, in the event that their child is murdered or arrested, often protest that their child led a wholesome life and that law enforcement is acting out of unfair motives by pursuing them. The trope makes fun of the women's weak defence of their children and is meant to be funny, though women in this situation are unlikely to find it so. Commenter's C contribution, the mention of 'buying scrap iron, old battery buying', would also be funny to Trinidadian readers, familiar with the call of scrapyard trucks which drive through residential areas purchasing these goods. Similarly, readers would also be amused trying to imagine a doubles vendor on the moon, doubles being a well-loved street food throughout the island. The initial humour presented by the original meme maker is thus elaborated upon by commenters.

(33) A: If we went to the moon, the craters would have potholes, the ship going back to earth would be dry docked and some gangster's mom would be yelling how them aliens too wicked
B: we would start planting weed and killing each other
C: and in the distance in the background: 'buying scrap iron, old battery buying'
D: And the doubles man

Viewed within the stringent standard language ideology of the gatekeepers in the comments in (33), it is possible to analyse the jocularity surrounding the memes with less generosity. In such a view, memes could be seen largely for their entertainment value and as a source of humour. They would share in the underlying standard language ideology and affirm the notion that Trinidadian English/Creole – and its speakers – cannot be taken seriously and deserve ridicule. There is an element of this in the data, as seen in the references to the speech on gang members' mothers in (33) and in the *Princess Margaret from Debe* memes, which, essentially, poke fun at a disadvantaged woman's attempt to preserve the natural environment in her community because of her language. As in the case of Jamaica's Clifton Brown's 'nobody canna cross it', in references to 'allyuh too wicked' and the *Princess Margaret* memes 'the object of humor is not the entextualized utterance itself anymore, but the speaker who first produced it' (Bohmann 2016: 145). While there is indeed both merit and necessity in taking such a critical view of the memes and the discourse surrounding them, it is important to simultaneously consider critical sociological insights into the role of humour in Trinidadian culture. Trinidad is known for its humour (Ilona 2005), which permeates its oral art forms such as calypso (Jones and Liverpool 1976; Mahabir 1996), its literature (Ilona 2005), and its social life and social media spheres (Sinanan 2017). Therefore, I think it is better to view humour in the memes largely as a form of picong.

A final aspect of language ideology that becomes apparent in the data is one which sees Trinidadian English/Creole as the acceptable norm and as something that is valuable and even prestigious. In the memes themselves this is relatively rare, but this ideology is present in the discourses surrounding them. This is seen by the frequent references to correctness that recur in the comments, in which participants acknowledge the Trinidadian English/Creole variant as the correct form or engage in discussions about what the form would be. In extracts (34)–(35), authority is given to the cat in the *Woman Yelling at Cat* meme. The cat's variant is legitimised by assertions of correctness for the cat who is 'never wrong' (34), 'correck' (35), and produces 'legit' speech (36). In (37), the commenter pronounces that the cat's language is the only acceptable way to speak, suggesting that, faced with British and American norms, Trinidadian norms are the 'only acceptable' variant.

(34) the cat is never wrong

(35) de cat is correck

(36) sounds legit

(37) the only acceptable way to speak

Trinidadian English/Creole, however, is still very much an emerging variety, and so acceptance of norms need not be equated with fixity of norms. Indeed, a number of exchanges in the comments show that, while users clearly prefer local variants, the exact forms are still negotiable. In (38), the four commenters respond to the meme creator's suggestion of *Gad-yan paper* ('Guardian paper' – sheets from the daily newspaper, *The Guardian*) for toilet paper. The first comment clarifies what the cat means: the meme maker has attempted to render the pronunciation of Guardian in eye dialect spelling. Speakers B and C, however, disagree with both the meme and Commenter A, arguing that the term is *gazette paper* (sheets of the now defunct *Port-of-Spain Gazette*), while D contributes another alternative, *outhouse paper*. Contributors B–D correct the others, their more knowledgeable stance marked by negators such as *nope* or the clause *you mean*.

(38) A: Guardian
B: Nope gazette
C: You mean gazette paper
D: You mean outhouse paper

Similarly, when a meme maker suggests that Trinidadians apologise by saying *hard lucks dey* (sorry about that), Commenter E (39) adds *padna** (partner) to the formulation, the use of the asterisk following *padna* a clear example of *-repair, which characterises self and other correction in written online language (Collister 2010). Commenter F supports this move, drawing on his individual expertise as a speaker of the variety to corroborate E's correction.

(39) E: hard lucks dey padna*
F: hard luck dey padna is exactly what I say

2.4 Conclusion

The language in Facebook memes and the discourse surrounding them is used to create a unified Trinidadian identity that is distinct from other national groups, particularly US Americans, British people, Guyanese, and Venezuelans. There is little tolerance for unratified variation within the speech community, and those whose language is perceived as differing too dramatically – Convent Girls and people who say 'my one' – are parodied as linguistic pariahs. Yet ideologies underlying such group formations are far from uniform. They are instead complex, and at times contradictory: Trinidadian English/Creole is simultaneously seen as being less than and/or equal to British and American English but superior to Guyanese English/Creole.

The key of the memes and most of the surrounding discussion is light-hearted and even frivolous; it is hardly possible to approach social media data without considering the notion of the ludic. Moreover, carnival and humour are at the core of the Trinidadian identity, and so the playfulness in the memes is in some ways unspectacular: more noteworthy would be its absence. Still, the humour belies the weighty work these memes undertake. Sociologically, they do point at potentially harmful racist, classist, and nationalistic ideologies that are encoded through language.

3 Identity and Ideologies in TikTok Videos

3.1 Introduction

On 25 May 2020, the TikToker RagaRebel/WelloNYC (Kwame Simpson) started a series of videos that would leave an indelible mark on the Caribbean social media landscape. Indeed, in an Instagram post two years later, the American-based Guyanese TikToker would acknowledge that 'two years ago today this video went viral and changed my life! I HAD THE CARIBBEAN IN A CHOKEHOLD TRU DI PANDEMIC AND IM FOREVER GRATEFUL!' (capitalisation in original). Simpson's *Letter of the Day* (*LoD*) format would be copied by fellow TikTokers DeShawn Wiggins of Barbados and Stephon Felmine of Trinidad and Tobago. The relationship between the subsequent videos is acknowledged by both TikTokers. In (40), Wiggins explains his motivation for the new content he is about to introduce and highlights that he would highlight Barbadian lexis.

(40) <DW>Hi uhm just wanted you guys to know that uhm I'll be recording a series similar to this guy's <#>What he does is explain Guyanese words through an alphabet system so I just figured it would be cool to do the same thing for Bajan words

Likewise, when, in his first post, Felmine is criticised for not adequately acknowledging the original maker of the *LoD* posts, he rebuts this, saying that he had indeed done so, a claim which is supported by another poster (41).

(41) User 1: hmmmmm. not original. u can give credit to the guyanese fella at least. Lol but i like that we getting a trini version
SF: ammm I did!!
User 2: He did . . . it's literally on the title post

Each of the content creators commits to producing twenty-six videos – one for each letter of the alphabet – though only Kwame Simpson and Stephon Felmine achieve this. Wiggins has technical difficulties at one point and, though he does resume, never gets to the end of the series. Felmine goes on to create subsequent series looking at numbers, idioms, Trinidad Carnival pronunciation, Bhojpuri, and Trinidad French Creole. This case study focusses on Felmine's first *LoD* series, referred to here as his English Creole series, but also considers his Bhojpuri and Trinidad French Creole series. The latter two are included since the lexical items he introduces in these alphabets are very often familiar to users because they have been borrowed into Trinidadian English Creole.

This section examines the *LoD* videos produced by the three TikTokers from May 2020 onwards. It considers how the content creators use language and other semiotic devices available to them to highlight aspects of their Caribbean identities and how ideologies about language in the Caribbean, and in their respective territories, are represented and reproduced in the videos. The section looks first at the structure and content of the videos before going on to look at how identity and ideological work is performed by the TikTokers.

3.2 The Letter of the Day Is . . .

The principal aim of the *LoD* series is to introduce viewers to vocabulary items that are specific to Guyana, Barbados, and Trinidad. To do so, the content creators use a format in which, each day, a new letter is introduced and explained to the viewers. The videos are therefore structurally similar. Each begins with an introduction in which the letter is introduced, followed by an example of the word beginning with the letter, its meaning, and its use in a sentence. The sequence then ends with the letter being repeated for the Barbadian and Trinidadian TikTokers, while Simpson repeats the lexical item. Examples of this structure for all three varieties can be seen in Table 2.

The influencers never stray from this script structure, and Felmine continues to adhere to it in the series he does on Trinidad French Creole and Trinbago Bhojpuri. The matrix language is English, though the examples are usually in Creole. Arguably, the use of a similar structure gives the elements that are different (e.g. *dumpsy*, *dangles*, *dongosorro*) a more marked status, highlighting the importance of differentiation and distinction in creating local identities in these videos. Felmine granted permission for his videos to be reproduced, and so the accompanying video for *dongosorro* can be viewed (see Video 1).

Table 3 documents the lexical items highlighted in the *LoD* series by all three TikTokers. The spellings used in the table, and throughout this section, are the

Table 2 The structure of the *Letter of the Day* (*LoD*) videos

	Barbados (Wiggins)	Guyana (Simpson)	Trinidad (Felmine)	Matrix language
Introduction	The letter of the day is D	The letter of the day is<,> D.	The letter of the day is<,> D	English
Letter	D is for dumpsy	D is for dangles	<#>D is for dongosorro	English
Meaning	Dumpsy is to be academically challenged or a phrase used to describe someone who is not doing well in school <#>Basically another word for retarded or slow	Dangles is when somebody is promiscuous [pɜrmɪskjuʌs] or little whory whory [ɔːri]	meaning you [jʊ] don't have any common sense	English and Creole
Example	<#>That big head child that Celeste got down the road like he<Creole>0</Creole> dumpsy <#>He<Creole>0</Creole> failing everything	<#>The girl with the arinj [arɪndʒ] halterback is dangles	<#>For example <#>My cousin <Creole>get</Creole> all his CXC and he <Creole>0</Creole> still dongosorro	Creole
Letter	<#>D	<#>Dangles	<#>D	

Table 3 Lexical items highlighted in the *LOD* videos

TikToker	*Items presented* (gloss in brackets)
Simpson	**English Creole:** *arinj* (orange), *blooshoom* (splash), *coongcy* (to defecate), *dangles* (promiscuous), *eyepass* (to disrespect), *farid* (forehead), *gyam* (to give), *hiyaga* (exclamatory warning), *iyodeez* (group), *jumbie* (ghost), *kangalang* (unprincipled person), *lamatuh* (slow or delayed), *mallybunta* (wasp), *nable* (belly button), *obeah* (witchcraft), *pattacake* (vagina), *quecumba* (cucumber), *rass* (buttocks), *skunt* (mother's private parts), *toelie* (penis), *usband* (husband), *voomvoom* (smell emanating from person's private parts), *whatax* (noise of a slap), *xamount* (quantity), *yatin* (plain sneaker), *zed* (zed)
Wiggins	**English Creole:** *afta* (after), *bruggadown* (broken), *chabakie* (the back of the head), *cawblen* (an expression of shock or disbelief), *dumpsy* (to be academically challenged), *evahsince* (used to exaggerate the passing of a length of time), *frowsy* (unpleasant smell), *goupma* (a really bad cough or cold), *horn* (to be unfaithful), *insi* (greeting), *Johnny* (a person with questionable intelligence)
Felmine	**English Creole:** *ah* (I), *braggadang* (old or in a state of disrepair), *cunumunu* (quiet or shy), *dongosorro* (lacking in common sense), *eh-heh* (really), *flamz* (to show off), *gyass* (indigestion), *heng* (to hang), *icenin* (icing), *jookin board* (scrubbing board), *kilketay* (to fall), *lickrish* (greedy), *mamaguy* (to sweet talk/ deceive), *nennen* (to face hard times), *obzockee* (awkward in appearance), *pickah* (thorns/fish bones), *quito quito* (very far), *raff* (to grab), *strims* (shrimp), *tusty* (desperate), *uppin* (to end a contract), *vampin* (to have an offensive odour), *warahoun* (a rowdy person), *x-tray* (x-ray), *yampee* (mucus in the corner of the eye), *zog-up* (to cut unevenly)
	Bhojpuri: *aajee* (paternal grandmother), *ai* (like this), *aray* (exclamation of surprise), *aunchie* (ritual healing), *ay* (exclamation), *baigan* (eggplant/aubergine), *bhaujee* (brother's wife), *chadar* (cheat), *chhachhunda* (a lout), *daaroo* (rum), *damaadol* (tomato), *dhakolay* (to guzzle), *dhoway* (to wash), *ee* (he/she/it), *gaaway* (to sing), *gheew* (clarified butter), *imlee* (tamarind), *jaadoo* (magic; obeah), *jhaaray* (to sweep; exorcise), *kaakee* (father's younger brother's wife), *kheesaa* (story), *laathee* (stick), *mamoo* (mother's brother), *naa* (no), *oochree* (mortar), *ortinee* (veil), *phasray* (to lounge), *poohar* (untidy/unkempt), *roti* (bread), *tarkaaree* (sautee), *terhee* (unwilling/stubborn), *thaapay* (pat down firmly), *thandaa* (cold), *ulloo* (owl; stupid person), *yag* (Hindu prayer meeting)
	French Creole: *afòs* (instensifier), *brave danjé* (recklessly brave), *chaplé* (string of prayer beads), *dingolé* (fall or tumble while dancing), *djèp* (wasp), *éti* (where), *èskizé mwen* (excuse me), *fèt* (party), *gwa Michel* (type of banana), *gwap* (bunch), *hale* (haul; pull), *I* (he/she/it), *jouvé*

Table 3 (cont.)

	(beginning of Carnival; daybreak), *kobo* (vulture), *lélé* (mix thoroughly), *move lang* (slanderous talk), *nòm* (man), *opò* (Port-of-Spain), *òlivé* (tree found in the forest), *potolégliz* (church pillar; regular churchgoer), *ramajé* (warbling of birds; dexterous instrumental performance), *samblé* (to gather coconuts or cocoa pods), *toutoulbé* (confused/foolish), *tjennèt* (small, green fruit), *vay ki vay* (careless and disorderly), *wi fout* (expression of surprise), *yonn* (one), *zanndoli* (lizard)

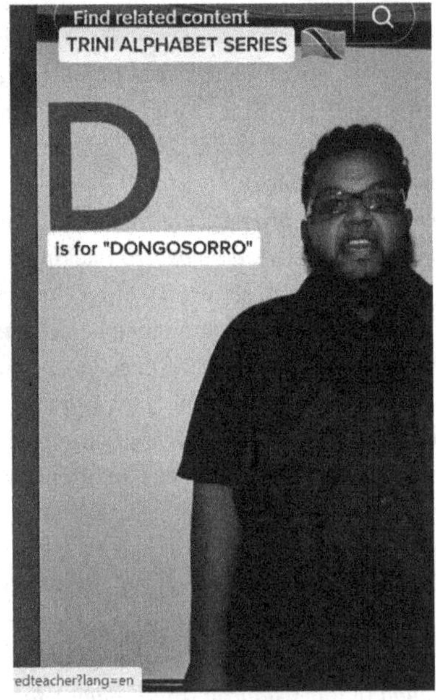

Video 1

Dongosorro (Courtesy Stephon Felmine) Video file and transcript available at www.cambridge.org/Guyanne

spellings that the TikTokers themselves employed. Focussing first on the English Creoles of the three territories, the first thing that becomes evident is that, although the content creators say they are focussing on vocabulary, they very often highlight phonological features of the varieties in question. This is particularly true of Kwame Simpson (Guyana) who highlights, for example, *arinj* (orange) and *farid* (forehead), which are in fact representative of the realisation of the LOT vowel as [a] in Guyanese Creole and are not separate lexical items. Other examples of pronunciation features in his vocabulary list are *nable* (navel, an exemplification of *b/v* alternation), *usband* (husband, an example of h-dropping) and *quecumba* (cucumber). Similarly, Stephon Felmine's addition of *ah* (I), *gyas* (gas), and *heng* (hang) highlight the Creole features of /g/ palatalisation (*gyas*) and stereotypical pronunciations of the other two items.

Another general observation to be made of the lists lies in the themes of the items chosen. A common theme used by all three TikTokers is that of stupid or foolish. In the Guyanese data, this is represented by the words *kangalang* (an unprincipled person) and *lamatuh* (a person who is slow or delayed). DeShawn Wiggins's inclusion of *dumpsy* (academically challenged) and *Johnny* (a stupid person) also belongs to this theme, as does Stephon Felmine's *cunumunu* (silly or stupid) and *dongosorro* (lacking in common sense). Another prominent theme is that of body parts and functions. The Trinidadian data contains three words belonging to this lexical field: *gyas* (stomach discomfort or indigestion); *vampin* (body odour), and *yampee* (mucus in the corner of the eyes). The lexical field of body parts and functions occurs four times in the Barbadian data with *chabakie*, meaning the back of a person's head; *frowsy*, meaning having an unpleasant smell; *goupma*, which refers to a cough or cold; and *horn*, meaning to be unfaithful to a partner in a monogamous relationship. The Guyanese TikToker identifies six words belonging to this theme, many of which might also be considered as taboo language, at least by more sensitive viewers and readers. These are *coongcy* (to defecate), *pattacake* (the female sexual organ), *rass* (buttocks), *toelie* (the male sexual organ), *skunt* (a person's mother's sexual organ, compare with English *cunt*), and *voomvoom* (unpleasant scents emanating from the male and female sexual organs). The inclusion of these items keys the Kwame Simpson videos as more markedly sexual than those of the other two posters.

One theme that is unique to Simpson is that of religion and belief, since only he includes the words *jumbie* and *obeah*, though Felmine does visit this theme in his Bhojpuri series with the inclusion of *jhaaray* (exorcise) and in his French Creole series with words such as *chaplé* (prayer beads). Felmine is the only TikToker to substantially address the theme of food and eating, with words such as *icenin* (icing), *pickah* (small bones in fish), and *lickrish* (greedy).

3.3 'I' Is for . . . Identity

TikTokers are involved in a quite intricate performance of identity in their videos. At a linguistic level, this is achieved through both speech and writing. Perhaps the most obvious claims that the TikTokers make are to national and regional identities, operationalised through the choice of vocabulary items unique, or believed to be unique, to the variety of English spoken in their territories. The items chosen must be distinct not only from British and American English vocabulary but also from other Caribbean varieties, and especially from the other varieties for which similar series exist. By and large, the TikTokers appear to achieve this since, as Table 3 shows, there is little overlap across the varieties in terms of the items chosen. In fact, only Barbadian *bruggadown* and Trinidadian *braggadang* appear to be similar, with a shared core meaning through the idea of being 'broken' or 'in a state of disrepair'. Indeed, it is not the case that the words selected are necessarily unique to the respective varieties. I consulted the *Dictionary of Caribbean English Usage* (Allsopp 2003) and the *Dictionary of the English/Creole of Trinidad and Tobago* (Winer 2009), as well as several folk dictionaries and glossaries, in order to gain insights into the territories in which the words might have originated and where they continue to be used. This search found that a number of items (*afta*, *bruggadown/braggadang*, *evahsince*, *horn*, *gyam*, *obeah*, *rass*, *ah cunumunu*, *eh-heh*, *icenin*, *jookin board*, *jumbie*, *lickrish*, *mamaguy*, *nennen*, *pickah*, *yampee*, *uppin*) are used in several territories and are not in fact unique to the variety at hand. In some cases, such as *mamaguy*, *nennen*, and *pickah*, all claimed by the Trinidadian TikToker Stephon Felmine, the other islands that make use of the words are neighbouring islands, such as Grenada, and so it is possible to account for this through contact and spread across the territories. But in other cases, such as *jumbie* and *obeah*, these words are attested in the entire region and are likely borrowings from West African languages. The sharedness of these features is also apparent in user comments, as seen in extracts (42)–(44). The first two comments are by users identifying as Jamaican commenting on the Barbadian series, while the third is an example of a person with considerable knowledge about lexical variation in Caribbean Englishes commenting on the Guyanese TikToks.

(42) Me a [emoji for Jamaica] finding these Caribbean words interesting

(43) Jamaicans say frowsy as well 😂😂😂😂

(44) Guyanese say Bragadam..Jamaicans say Radam . . . .Trinis say Kilkaytay all meaning the same thing 😂😂😂😂😂😂😂😂😂

Conferral with dictionaries and glossaries also made it possible to examine the extent to which the words chosen have been recorded formally. This is seen in Figure 30. In Figure 30, words coded Dictionary were found in a dictionary or glossary with the same (or at least a very similar) meaning as the one used by the TikToker, while words labelled TikTok only comprised words that could not be found in any dictionary or glossary. Words labelled 'other' comprised a small group of words that were found in the dictionary but with a meaning or spelling

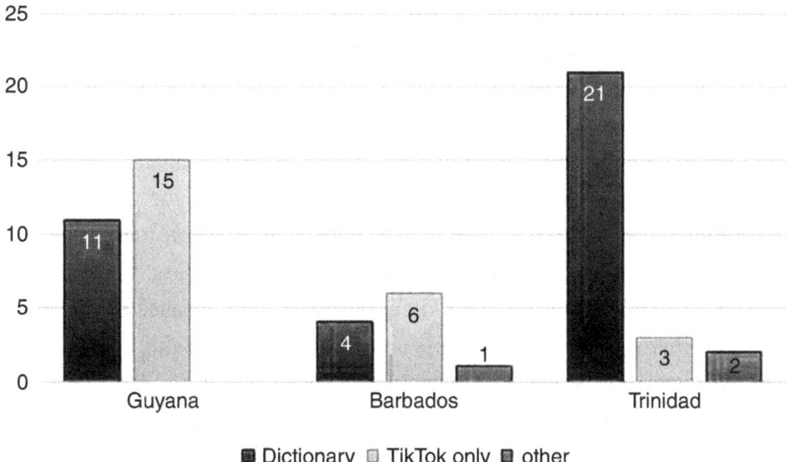

Figure 30 Occurrence of lexical items in dictionaries and glossaries across varieties

substantially different from the one the TikToker gave. Figure 30 shows that eleven of the twenty-six words presented by Simpson appear in any dictionary or glossary, while fifteen do not. One word, *mallybunta*, presents problem for categorisation. The *Dictionary of Caribbean English Usage* lists the word as *marabunta* but gives the same meaning as Simpson does (a wasp). Therefore, this was seen as just a difference in pronunciation, and subsequently spelling. A similar pattern can be seen in the Barbadian data, in which only four of the words appear in any dictionary, though a further word, *dumpsy*, appears with an alternative spelling and pronunciation. Interestingly, in the original TikTok, Wiggins does provide both spellings in the visual frame but only ever uses the pronunciation [dɒmpsi:]. The words that are not accounted for in any dictionary or glossary are *chabakie*, *cawblen*, *goupma*, *insi*, and *Johnny*. In contrast to his Caribbean neighbours, most of Stephon Felmine's Trinidadian lexical items (twenty-one out of twenty-six) are accounted for in either of the two dictionaries consulted. Three – *tusty*, *heng*, and *flamz* – do not appear at all, while the final two words – *braggadang* and *uppin* – appear with different meanings. The difference in these frequencies across the three TikTokers, however, may be due to the fact that Winer's (2009) work is a comprehensive and definitive dictionary of the English/Creole of Trinidad and Tobago but a work of similar scope and scholarship does not exist for either of the other varieties.

It is perhaps useful to examine the words that only appear on TikTok and are not attested in other, more formal repositories of English. For Guyanese English and Creole, words that did not appear in any written record included words which Simpson had added based on their pronunciation, such as *arinj* (orange), *farid* (forehead), and *usband* (husband). These items highlight features of Guyanese pronunciation: the realisation of LOT as [a] in *arinj* and *farid* and the phenomenon of h-dropping as in *usband*. This is also true of the Trinidadian *heng*, which represents the Creole pronunciation of the word *hang*. Interestingly, however, Winer's dictionary does include *ketch*, meaning catch, in which the vowel arguably has undergone the same process. For Wiggins, examples of words that have most likely been included because of pronunciation rather than lexical distinctiveness are *cawblen* and *insi*, which captures the glottal pronunciation of the final element of the greeting.

Other words that do not appear in dictionaries are words that could be considered as slang or taboo. These include *pattacake* (vagina), *toelie* (penis), *skunt* (mother's vagina), and *voomvoom* (scent emanating from a person's private parts). However, two of these words do appear in online sources such as Urban Dictionary. *Pattacake* is also the focus of an April 2019 YouTube video by the Guyanese YouTuber Guyana Uncut, and a Google search for *skunt* leads to the opportunity to buy T-shirts and sweatshirts with the word emblazoned across them via Amazon, marketed as 'custom designed Skunt slang design for Guyanese who are patriotic and loves their roots and country as well as the loud vocabulary'. Such items of clothing are popular in all three territories and, as Johnstone (2013) has noted for Pittsburghese, serve to enregister and commodify the variety. For the Guyanese examples, their attestation in other online sources and on clothing suggests that the terms are familiar to other Guyanese English and Creole speakers and underscores the authenticity of the TikToker's identity claims.

The Trinidadian TikToker tends to steer away from such taboo language, with the possible exception of *tusty*, which has the meaning of being desperate. Although it is not recorded in the *Dictionary of the English/Creole of Trinidad and Tobago*, the term does appear in popular culture. It is recorded in the Urban Dictionary, which attributes it to the 2009 song *Tusty* by soca artiste Blaxx, in which he sings: '*Ah tusty fuh wine mama / Ah tusty to grind mama*' (I'm desperate to dance with gyrating movement, lady / I'm desperate to dance, lady).

Tusty is also attested in other scholarly literature. In their digital-anthropological study of images on Facebook, Miller and Sinanan (2017) report on one participant who, upon seeing one of their visual stimuli, comments that the person in the picture looks *tusty*. They go on to write that: 'She explained "well, the expression could be said like a dog who panting for water. So they use it for guys who running down women, like thirsty for women. So he saying there are so many 'tusty' guys on Facebook"' (Miller and Sinanan 2017: 187).

Their participant's explanation matches the one given by Felmine in his videos. If the folk etymology given in Urban Dictionary is correct, and the first real attestation of this item is Blaxx's song, then this would explain why it does not appear in Winer's dictionary of the same year, since the data collection for this work would have been completed by that point. *Flamz* does not appear in any subsequent searches online. One way to account for its inclusion might be that Felmine is a secondary school teacher and his contact with young people may have brought him into contact with slang which is unknown to the broader speech community and which is not typically included in dictionaries.

In highlighting vocabulary felt to be unique to their territories, the TikTokers position themselves as particularly knowledgeable about the language varieties spoken there. Local identity, be it Barbadian, Guyanese, or Trinidadian, is performed through the influencers' choice of lexical items. They choose words that are unique, or at least perceived to be unique, to that variety and, as Table 3 shows, they not only present the words but also the spellings and meanings of the words and examples of them being used in a sentence. For forms that occur in other varieties of English, such as *frowsy* and *Johnny* in the Barbadian videos, this contextual information is critical since it highlights the particular use of a word in that variety and how it is different from other uses of the same form. In this way, local identity work involves a measure of language ownership since local meanings are legitimised and spread.

The use of lexical items is not limited to words being highlighted. Throughout the videos, particularly in the example section, the TikTokers draw on other lexical items associated with the region, or with the specific variety. For instance, (45) contains the Trinidadian lexical items *too-too* (defecate) and *sou-sou* (a local savings programme).

(45) <$SF><#>The letter of the day is<,> A <#>A stands for ah and it is used instead of I <#>For example <#>Ah want to <word>too-too</word> <#>Ah thief me neighbour fowl <#>Ah want to join the <word>sou-sou</word> <#>A

Similarly, (46) contains the Guyanese lexical item *boungee* (bump or boil).

(46) <$KS><#>A bai tek he eye an pass me <#>I had to send he home with a <word>boungee</word> <Creole>[an]</Creole> he farid

Beyond the lexical items, the TikTokers' claims to Caribbean identities are established through their use of other linguistic features of Caribbean Englishes, notably the grammar and pronunciation used. In terms of grammatical features,

TikTokers typically employ features that are shared across Caribbean Englishes and Creoles, rather than those specific to their own territories. These include the use of zero past tense markers as seen in (47)–(49), where the speakers recount an event in the past but the verbs *move off* (drive off), *get*, *fall down* (fall), *thief* (steal), and *make* do not receive any past tense morphological marker.

(47) <$DW><#><Creole>[di]</Creole> driver for <Creole>[di]</Creole> Bascobel bus <Creole>move off</Creole> before <Creole>I get my seat</Creole> and Bruggadown <#><Creole>I fall down</Creole>

(48) <$SF><#>Or <#>Shanti <Creole>stop</Creole> getting <Creole>invite</Creole> to <Creole>wedding</Creole> and <word>prayers</word> because she <Creole>0</Creole> too lickrish

(49) <$KS>A <Creole>[baɪ]</Creole> coongcy <Creole>make</Creole> blooshoom in the <Creole>[taɪlɛt]</Creole>

Similarly, in the examples (50)–(51) zero third-person singular -s agreement can be seen in the constructions *(the girl) smell*, *she don't*, and *Shirley like*.

(50) <$DW><#><Creole>[dat]</Creole> girl Shakira that's get in the number ten van always <Creole>smell</Creole> frowsy <#>She <Creole>don't</Creole> bathe

(51) <$SF><#><#>Shirley <Creole>like</Creole> to flamz <Creole>she buss-up</Creole> dress in the <Creole>[di]</Creole> gallery <Creole>[gjalɐri]</Creole>

The final feature of the verb phrase that is evident in the TikTok data is the use of copula and auxiliary deletion. This is seen in (52) and (53) where the markup <Creole>0</Creole> highlights the slot into which the auxiliary form *are* might be inserted in other varieties of English.

(52) <$DW><#><Creole>0</Creole> You sure you got Goupma or covid <#>You <Creole>0<Creole> coughing real bad <#>Goupma

(53) <$SF><#>People <Creole>0</Creole> catching <Creole>[keʧɪn] [de]</Creole> nennen <Creole>[di:z]</Creol> days for <Creole>[wʌk]</Creole>

Beyond the verb phrase, several features of the Caribbean Creole noun phrase are present in the data. The first of these concerns the formation of plurals. TikTokers use zero plural marking, as in (54), in which the noun *lime* is not pluralised, although it seems fairly obvious based on the context that the speaker does not wish to steal only one lime. Caribbean Creoles also form plurals by adding the suffix *-dem*, and an example of this is seen in (55) when Simpson uses *eyebrow dem*, the Creole equivalent of English *eyebrows*.

(54) <$SF><#>When I <Creole>go</Creole> to <Creole>[ti:f di:]</Creole> [di] <Creole>neighbour lime</Creole> pickah well jook me

(55) <$KS><#>Farid is a part of <Creole>[də]</Creole> face above <Creole>di</Creole> <Creole>eyebrow dem</Creole>

Another feature of Caribbean Creole noun phrase usage which occurs in the data is the use of British English subject pronouns in object position or as possessive determinatives. In (51), for instance, *she* is the determinative occurring before *buss-up dress* in the noun phrase *she buss-up dress* (her ripped dress) and (56) contains an instance of subject pronoun *they* being used as a possessive determiner in *they eyes* (their eyes).

(56) <$KS><#>Eyepass or when somebody <Creole>tek</Creole> <Creole>they</Creole> eyes and pass you

Furthermore, there are examples of British English object pronouns as determinatives, as seen in (57), in which English *them*, realised with an initial stop, precedes *people* in *dem people* (those people).

(57) <$DW><#>You know <Creole>[dɛm]</Creole> people <Creole>is</Creole> talk

The final key feature of the noun phrase in the data is the use of adjacency to show possession, which is seen in the phrase 'Susan phone bill' (58), in which the possessor, *Susan*, and the possessed, *phone bill*, are placed next to each other.

(58) <$SF><#>Or when Digi-hell cut <Creole>Susan phone bill</Creole> she <Creole>gone</Creole> in there and <Creole>get on</Creole> like a real warahoun

Another level at which linguistic identity is performed in the data is through the use of Creole pronunciations. In the first instance, this is seen through words that are highlighted not because they are unique lexically but because their pronunciation sets them apart. For Guyana, these are the words *arinj*, *usband*, *farid*, and *quecumba*; for Trinidad, they are *heng*, *gyas*, *strims*, and *x-tray*; and for Barbados, they are *afta* and *evahsince*. In the case of the Trinidadian examples, *strims and x-tray* have in fact been codified and are included in Winer's (2009) dictionary. Additionally, TikTokers make use of phonological features common to Caribbean Creoles and, at times, features that are unique to their own varieties. Creole pronunciations are often contained within the examples, with the other parts of the videos usually using English variants. By far the most common feature upon which the TikTokers draw is the realisation of British English dental fricatives as stops. Examples of this can be seen in each of the TikTokers' speech and occur for both the voiced and voiceless variants. This can be seen in (59)–(61), in which each of the TikTokers uses TH-stopping. Kwame Simpson uses it in the words *these* ([di:z]) and *they* ([de]), with the latter example also being used by DeShawn Wiggins (60). The examples from Stephon Felmine's videos contain both voiceless and voiced variants with *thief the* realised as [ti:f di].

(59) <$KS><#>These hardback cockroach [di:z] [ardbak] [kakaroʧ] really take their [tɛk] [de] eyes and [an] pass we

(60) <$DW><#>They must be [de] [mʌs] be [kɔmɪn] back for that six feet set she take [tɛk] out

(61) <$SF><#><#><#>You <Creole>eh</Creole> (didn't) hear is a soldier who thief the [ti:f di] money up La Horquetta girl [gjʌl] <#>Eh-heh <#>You <Creole>eh</Creole> hear Rowley cancel Carnival [kjanivʌl] next year girl [gjɜ:l]

(62) <$SF><#>My neighbour making [mekɪn] a whole set of old [o:l] noise with <Creole>he</Creole> braggadang car

Another consonantal feature that TikTokers employ in their speech is the use of consonant cluster reduction. This is seen in (59) in Kwame Simpson's pronunciation of *and* as [an], DeShawn Wiggins's realisation of *must* as [mʌs] (60), and Stephon Felmine's realisation of *old* as [o:l] (62). Relatedly, the TikTokers frequently realise [ɪŋ] as [ɪn], as seen in the examples of *coming* in (60) and *making* in (62).

In terms of vowels, one feature that occurs in videos by all three TikTokers is the use of [ɛ] in TRAP and FACE contexts, resulting in pronunciations such as [mɛk], [tɛk], and [kɛʧ]. This is seen in (59)–(62) for all three TikTokers, with Kwame Simpson and DeShawn Wiggins both using the pronunciation [tɛk] for *take* and Stephon Felmine producing *making* as [mɛkɪn]. For Felmine, this is also demonstrated in the selection of *heng* as one word in his alphabet. It should be noted that it does not appear to be the case that this pronunciation can be applied to all words. For example, *back* in extract (60) is pronounced as [bak].

The examples in (59)–(62) also highlight pronunciation features that individual TikTokers employ that are not drawn upon by others. For Kwame Simpson (59), this comprises the use of h-dropping, as seen in his pronunciation of the word *hardback* as [ardbak]. He also uses [a] in LOT, as seen in the pronunciation of *cockroach* as [kakaro:ʧ]. Elsewhere, he uses [aɪ] in the CHOICE lexical setting, resulting in pronunciations such as [baɪ] for *boy.* Only DeShawn Wiggins of Barbados uses glottal stops, but both he and Simpson use rhotic pronunciations.

This is in keeping with general descriptions of both varieties. Stephon Felmine often palatalises velar stops, so that /k/ and /g/ become [kj] and [gj] in his speech, as seen in his pronunciation of *girl* and *carnival* in (61) as [gjʌl] (also [gjɜ:l]) and [kjanivʌl]. Moreover, TikTokers sometimes engage in one-off pronunciations that serve as identity markers since they mark the stereotypical pronunciation of a word. This is best seen in Stephon Felmine's pronunciation of *September* as [sɛktɛmbɐ]. This pronunciation is even commented upon by several posters, with one asking, 'is sectember u say dey??? or I hearing wrong . . . 😏😅😄'.

There are, in contrast, features of individual varieties that occur fairly regularly in the videos but cannot really be argued to be doing any identity work, since there does not appear to be any systematic variation in how these features are used. While the use of fricatives versus stops does appear to be doing real identity work (see Figure 31), this is not the case for other features. For example, in the Barbadian data, DeShawn Wiggins uses a glottal stop in eight of the eleven contexts where it could be used and, though this helps establish his speech as a Barbadian, there is no evidence that he is intentionally drawing on this feature in his performance of identity. This is also true of his use of rhotic pronunciations, which he employs in twenty-six of the twenty-nine phono-opportunities for the feature. Similarly, Kwame Simpson's use of [aɪ] in CHOICE contexts is categorical, as is his use of [a:] in THOUGHT, with his use of [a] in LOT being near categorical (eighteen out of twenty tokens). His consistent use of these variants allows him to be identified as a speaker of Guyanese English/Creole but is not necessarily part of his performance of the variety. That being said, the co-occurrence of such non-stylised language use makes the TikTokers' use of language seem authentic and marks them as genuine speakers of Caribbean Creoles.

Indeed, it is not simply the occurrence of the individual lexical, phonological, and grammatical forms that allow the TikTokers to perform their Caribbean identities. Rather, it is the co-occurrence of forms and, in particular, their location in the examples. This practice is reflected in the structure of the videos, as was seen in Table 2. The matrix language, that is, the language in which the discourse is framed, is largely English, with Creole only appearing in the example section of the discourse. The Guyanese TikToker also uses Creole in the definition frame and in general is more fluid in his language use between frames, but for the Barbadian and Trinidadian TikTokers the pattern above holds true for all of their posts. Indeed, for Stephon Felmine the phrase *For example* tends to represent a change in footing (Goffman 1979) and is used to introduce the examples in all of his videos. This consistency can be seen by comparing Table 2 to (63).

(63) <$SF><#>The letter of the day is L <#>L is for lickrish meaning very greedy <#>For example <#>My lickrish uncle <Creole>pack up</Creole> all the food in <Creole>box</Creole> before anybody could eat <#>Or <#>Shanti <Creole>stop</Creole> getting <Creole>invite</Creole> to <Creole>wedding</Creole> and <Creole>prayers</Creole> because she <Creole>0</Creole> too lickrish <#>L

Once more, the language before the example is English but afterwards Creole features appear. Felmine's *for example* attunes listeners to his discourse and prepares them for the Creole speech that will follow. Indeed, several viewers comment on the importance of *for example* in marking the change of footing with comments such as those in (64) and (65).

(64) Is how he does say 'for example' (It's how he says 'for example')

(65) is how sir does be well serious when he saying 'For example' (It's how Sir is very serious when he's saying 'For example').

The concentration of Creole phonological features is also higher after the change of footing, that is, in the example, than elsewhere. This is particularly true for the Barbadian and Trinidadian TikTokers, as is illustrated in Figure 31. The figure shows the occurrence of stop and fricative realisations in the videos for all tokens of words containing <TH> that would be pronounced with a voiced or voiceless fricative in standard British or American English. There were 247 tokens in total, with Barbados having fewer tokens than the other varieties due to the fact that Wiggins only went up to J. Focussing first on the

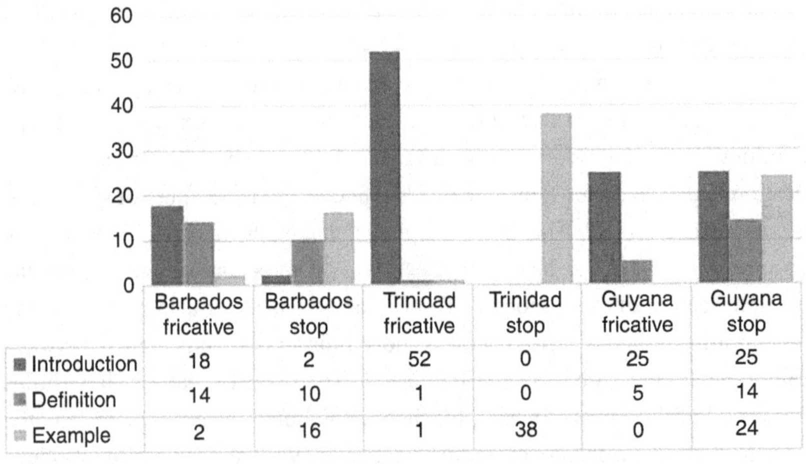

	Barbados fricative	Barbados stop	Trinidad fricative	Trinidad stop	Guyana fricative	Guyana stop
Introduction	18	2	52	0	25	25
Definition	14	10	1	0	5	14
Example	2	16	1	38	0	24

Figure 31 Distribution of TH- fricatives and stops in Caribbean TikTok videos

'Introduction' and 'Example' segments of the videos, the figure suggests that there is a clear sense of stylistic variation between these two sections for the TikTokers, particularly for Wiggins (Barbados) and Felmine (Trinidad). In both cases, there seems to be a clear division of labour for stops and fricatives; fricatives appear almost categorically in the introductions of both varieties, eighteen times in Wiggins's speech and fifty-two times in Felmine's, but are almost completely absent from the examples – just twice in Wiggins's speech and once in Felmine's. In contrast, stops occur more frequently in the Barbadian examples than in the introductions, and Stephon Felmine uses stops categorically in his examples. The categorical use of stops in the examples is also seen in Kwame Simpson's TikToks, but, unlike the other two, he shows an equal use of fricatives and stops in the introduction. Nevertheless, the complete absence of fricatives in the examples does have the overall effect of making the introduction to the videos sound more standard and formal than the later parts.

Finally, the TikTokers make identity claims through their use of language to construct shared social and background knowledge contexts for themselves and their viewers. The former is achieved through the overall framing of the discourse. The TikTokers imagine themselves as teachers, making their viewers pupils, a role which viewers seem happy to accept. In the Barbadian data, one follower comments that Wiggins is the 'BEST. TEACHER.EVA.' The Trinidadian TikToker Stephon Felmine is in fact a teacher, and TikTokers identify as members of his classroom community, referring to him as *Sir* and wishing him Happy Teachers Day, commenting on the pedagogical value of the videos in comments such as 'uwi could use u for creole linguistics class yes', and even associating him with the Trinidad and Tobago Unified Teachers' Association (TTUTA), 'TTUTA [Trinidad and Tobago emoji] better give this teacher an Award!' The TikTokers are not only teachers but teachers in Caribbean schools, and their overall use of language recreates Caribbean education contexts in which English may be used to frame a lesson but Creole is used for more interactive elements (Deuber 2009: 98). As has been demonstrated, the distribution of Creole and English forms in the videos mimics this classroom interaction pattern. At the same time, as Singh (2023), writing on Simpson's and Felmine's videos, notes, the juxtaposition of colloquial language in a setting in which formal language is socially expected is the source of the videos' humour.

In addition to these acts of framing, *LoD* producers create a shared background information context by referring to places and public figures with whom they assume their followers to be familiar. The assumption of shared knowledge – and its successful uptake by the viewers – is critical to the claim not just to an identity but to an authentic identity. Thus, when DeShawn Wiggins refers to specific parishes in Barbados (St Lucy and St John), bus routes (Boscobel, St Patrick's, number 10), public figures such as Jenkins, financial practices such as the repossession of goods by the Courts furniture company, and stereotypes surrounding the alleged unfaithfulness in monogamous relationships by 'members of BDF [Barbadian Defence Force] members of the Coast Guard, van men footballers, cricketers, DJs, women from St John, and men from St Joseph', he establishes himself as a real Barbadian, aware of the quotidian experiences of his fellow Barbadians. The mention of specific parishes elicits some reactions from Wiggins's followers, who, for example, defend the residents of St John saying, 'What St. John people do you!?! 😂😂😂' and 'lmao how dare he mention the st John women 😁😁😁😁😁😁'.

Similarly, Stephon Felmine's videos contain references to places in Trinidad (La Horquetta, Queen Street), companies (T&TEC, Digi-hell, a play on the word Digicel, Jimmy Aboud); rites of passage and cultural institutions (CXC, a reference to the Caribbean Examinations Council, but actually how people refer to the Caribbean Secondary Examination Certificate exams colloquially; sou-sou, a means of community savings; wedding and prayers; OJT (the government's on-the-job training programme); current events (the prime minister cancelling Carnival); and public figures (Rowley – an informal but common way of referring to the prime minister). In his decision to use the expressions that other Trinidadians normally employ in their everyday communication, for example by not referring to the prime minister as Dr Keith Rowley or to OJT and CXC by their more formal names, Felmine is able to make claims to an authentic Trinidadian identity.

Finally, both Felmine and Wiggins use fictitious names as a way of claiming identity and affiliation with their followers. Wiggins does this sparingly and exercises great caution in this regard. For example, after using the girl's name Shakira in his example for *frowsy*, he breaks the fourth wall and says 'If there's a Shakira on the number ten route I am so sorry'. This stepping out of character suggests that Shakira is a common enough name in Barbados that there could hypothetically be a Shakira who takes the number ten bus and who might be offended. Felmine, however, has no such qualms and regularly uses names in his videos, particularly names associated with Indo-Trinidadian heritage, such as *Lalchan*, *Meena*, and *Shanti*, though he also uses names not affiliated with any particular ethnic group, such as *Natalia* and *Kelly*. The use of names, as well as real or imagined family members, allows the followers to sympathise with the exploits Felmine invents for them, as seen in contributions such as 'Poor Shanti' and 'aye your uncle smart'. Most notably, in the example for T, 'Since Natalia getting older, she getting more tusty for a man' (As Natalia gets older, she's getting more desperate for a man), ten commentors of the twenty-five used in the sample jump to Natalia's defence, saying 'how that looking like you throwing words for Natalia so' (Why does it seem as though you're accusing Natalia indirectly?) and 'How yuh could do Natalia that Teach?' (How can you do that to Natalia?). A further six Natalias mockingly protest the use of their name, with one even adding, 'Ah not tusty fuh no man eh 😂🤣😂🤣😂' (I'm not desperate for a man). In this way, the use of names allows the TikToker and his followers to create affective bonds, however intangible these may be.

In contrast to the Barbadian and Trinidadian TikTokers, Simpson does not ever refer to specific place names or events in Guyana in his TikTok videos. Moreover, he refrains from using names in his examples, instead using more generic markers such as 'a boy', 'somebody', and 'gyal' (girl). Though his pronunciation of these items does mark him as Guyanese, it could be argued that, in not using actual names and places from Guyana, Simpson fails to take advantage of possible contextual features that might add a layer of authenticity to his videos.

3.3.1 Identity in Writing

Though the lion's share of identity work in the videos is done via speech, as a multimodal platform, written language plays a crucial role in the performance of identities on TikTok. Identity is displayed through the direct naming of countries and territories by the TikTokers. In the videos by DeShawn Wiggins and Stephon Felmine, the words 'Bajan alphabet' and 'Trini alphabet series' appear on the screen for each of the videos. In this way, the content creators continuously signal their national identity and invite viewers who may claim affiliation with these identities to follow their content. Moreover, in the video descriptions, DeShawn Wiggins includes the hashtags #bajanalphabet, #bajan, #tiktokbarbados, #bajantiktok, and #caribbean, while Stephon Felmine uses #trinidad, #trinitiktoker, and the subscript TT after the video caption. Simpson's videos do not contain any similar headings in the content of the video, though the video captions do contain the hashtags #guyanesetiktok, #westindiantiktok, and #caribbeantiktok. Previous research on identity on social media has consistently shown how hashtags are an important means through which users can establish 'affiliation via "findability"' (Zappavigna 2011: 789) since they allow social media to become searchable. Hashtags therefore can be employed to signal identification, affiliation, membership, and shared beliefs and values, as the Caribbean content creators seem to do, thereby highlighting their national and regional identities. In this regard, that Felmine does not include a hashtag referring to the Caribbean is noteworthy. It perhaps suggests that his content is targeted almost exclusively to Trinidadian users of the platform – he even excludes Tobago in his first series. Indeed, although in the subsequent series on Bhojpuri and Trinidad French Creole he employs the blend 'Trinbago', he never adds Tobago to his list of hashtags, which seems to indicate a strong identification with Trinidad separate from Tobago and from the wider Caribbean. The other TikTokers, however, claim not only a national identity but also a broader Caribbean identity through their use of hashtags.

Written language is also an important means through which followers are able to express their identity. This is seen especially in the comments. The very act of commenting on the videos can be seen as an act of identity since, in doing so, the contributor is presenting themself as a legitimate addressee of the original video, with the attendant right to contribute to the discourse. More specifically, written contributions allow commentors to perform national identity and regional in three key ways. The first way in which this is achieved is through making direct identity claims, in which commentors share their own status as citizens of the territory, either resident there or in the diaspora. This is seen in (66), in which the respondent claims to be from one of the parishes Wiggins mentions in his videos (St John). Likewise, in (67), the user comments that they are from Trinidad and confirms that 'everyone' uses the word that Felmine has proffered.

(66) I'm from St John murder 😁

(67) I from trinidad and everybody does say that 😁😁😁😁

Further to these direct claims, identity is also performed through the use of pronominal forms, especially first-person plural forms such as *we*, *us*, and *our*. These forms suggest inclusion and point to the poster's identification as a member of a group. For instance, in (68), the contributor's use of 'we' shows that they consider themselves to be a member of the community whose language is being described.

(68) Ah weak 😁😁😁😁😁 we really does use that word for a lot of different meanings

In addition to this, posters also make use of first-person singular forms to show a level of individual identity. The poster in (69), for example, aligns themselves with the word by claiming to use it frequently.

(69) 😁😁😁 OMG! I say that alllll the time!

3.3.2 Beyond the National: Ethnic Identities in Stephon Felmine's Videos

In addition to videos highlighting the Creole and English of the territories, Stephon Felmine also produces videos in which other languages of Trinidad and Tobago are highlighted: Trinbago French Creole (Patois) and Trinbago

Bhojpuri. In each of these series, different aspects of identity are highlighted. The most marked change to the identity claims in the latter two series is seen in the title and hashtags. Whereas before Felmine only claimed affiliation with Trinidad, in the Patois and Bhojpuri series the blend Trinbago is used. The structure of the videos is otherwise essentially unchanged, with one minor addition within the introductory section of the Introduction–Word–Announcement of example–Example structure. Because the letters of the day are unfamiliar to the viewers, Felmine also demonstrates how they ought to be pronounced before continuing with the representative lexical item.

In terms of writing, Felmine's ethnic identity is particularly marked in the Bhojpuri videos. These videos contain examples of the Devanagari script, illustrating how both the letter of the day and its attendant word are written, as seen in Figure 32. These are followed by the Roman script representation of the words. The Devanagari script is presented on the left and, since literacy practices in Trinidad and Tobago are based on English and therefore viewers are likely to read from left to right, this information is one of the first things viewers encounter on opening the video. However, given the overall low rates of literacy in Hindi and/or Bhojpuri in Trinidad and Tobago, the use of this script is almost entirely symbolic and serves to underscore Indo-Trinidadian-ness.

Figure 32 Trinbago Bhojpuri letter of the day (Courtesy Stephon Felmine)

Furthermore, although the earliest videos do not include it, later videos, such as Figure 32, do include the Caribbean Hindustani logo in the bottom-left corner. Hindustani is written in Samarkan font, which aesthetically resembles the Devanagari script but uses Roman letters. Caribbean Hindustani is only spoken by small populations in Trinidad, Guyana, and Suriname, and so the mention of Caribbean rather than Trinbagonian is an act of affiliation with a broader Indo-Caribbean identity that is also not present in the original *LoD* videos.

Lack of familiarity with Bhojpuri and Patois means that, for the viewers, too, the ways in which identity is performed in writing are different from in the English and Creole *LoD* videos. The act of seeking out and viewing the videos is an act of identity, and one in which fewer people engage than in the original series. Moreover, while in the English and Creole videos identity could be performed by claiming knowledge of the words, this is rarely the case for the Bhojpuri and Patois words. Where this is done, commentors appear both pleased and surprised by their knowledge of a word. Instead, identity is performed through demonstrated willingness to learn about the languages and by acknowledging ignorance of lingua-cultural capital.

Moreover, identity work and affiliation are done by showing approval of Felmine's project and affection for the alphabet series. The commenter in (70) is an example of the many who express love for the series, while the one in (71) represents the many comments that highlight the educational value of the series. The contribution by the commentor in (71) is particularly notable since the commenter also highlights the country name.

(70) Omg loving this patois series!

(71) I can't believe that Trini vernacular language derived from Patois! Your videos are not only funny but educational!

This does not mean that viewers never have knowledge of the words, and with lexical items that have been borrowed and are well established in Trinidadian English and Trinidadian Creole, viewers perform identity in several ways. One of these is by claiming expert knowledge through challenging Felmine's spelling of a word. In (72), the user compares their spelling of *bhaigan* to the one Felmine uses (*baigan*), with the face-saving addendum of 'I could be wrong'.

(72) i doh spell it so i does spell it like bhaigan idk i could be wrong

Similarly, one user replies to Felmine's spelling of *fèt* (for *fete*, meaning party) by first asking for confirmation on the anglicised spelling of the word and then, as with the user in the previous extract, saves face by claiming to have spelled the word incorrectly their whole life (73).

(73) Is not fete? I was spelling this thing wrong my whole life boy

Expert status might also be performed by avowed usage of the word and expanding on the explanation the TikToker gives. For instance, in (74) the contributor highlights their own Indo-Trinidadian identity by claiming to use the word *aajee* and showing that they know the difference between *aajee* (father's mother) and *nani* (mother's mother).

(74) I say dat and nani is ur mothers mother

However, not all users attend to Felmine's (and their own) face needs to this extent. The commentor in (75), for instance, corrects the spelling *gwa Michel* and includes and admonition to *get it right.*

(75) Gros Michel. get it right

Finally, identity work is done by the viewers who identify iconic speakers of the varieties. Very often, these are grandparents, with comments such as that in (76) scattered throughout the comments section.

(76) Yes. Yes. My granny use to say this

Elsewhere, the commenters identify people who should be iconic speakers but who reject the linguistic forms associated with that identity. In (77), older women, who the commenter believes ought to identify as Indo-Trinidadian, eschew Bhojpuri forms of address in favour of English ones.

(77) Nowadays the Aajee don't want to be called Aajee 😏 they telling the child 'call me Grandma' [thinking face emoji] 😂

3.3.3 Non-linguistic Acts of Identity in the LoD *Videos*

One important means through which TikTokers perform identity is through the use of props and settings. In the videos, the content creator recreates a prototypical classroom setting, presenting themselves as schoolteachers standing in front of a real or virtual board and, in the case of the Guyanese and Trinidadian influencers, armed with a ruler that they use to point at the letter of the day. The ruler is reminiscent of corporal punishment, which was a regular feature of Caribbean schooling at least until the turn of the century and establishes the violent authority of the teacher figure in Caribbean classrooms. Moreover, in as far as teachers were, at least historically, viewed as language experts, modelling standardised English and providing norms of English usage (see Deuber 2009; Devonish and Thomas 2012: 181; Hackert 2016: 88), the decision to set the videos in a simulated classroom environment allows the influencers to, wittingly or unwittingly, claim an expert identity. However, unlike traditional teachers, who use, or are at least expected to use, standardised Caribbean varieties (see Meer et al. 2019; Hänsel et al. 2022), TikTok teachers model Creole.

Non-linguistic performances of identity are also achieved through the use of clothing. Throughout his series, Kwame Simpson sports a large handkerchief with an imprint of the Guyanese flag, which he usually wears as a necktie, though sometimes he wears it as a belt. The other two TikTokers do not do this, though DeShawn Wiggins is sometimes clad in the colours of the Barbadian national flag. In this way, both Simpson and Wiggins subtly signal their national identity outwardly. Stephon Felmine does not do this, at least not at a national level, though his clothing does generate a great deal of discourse among followers. Felmine changes his shirt every day, and while some of them are plain polo shirts, many of them are flashy shirts with gaudy designs. In this way, Felmine's dress style has some parallels to earlier saga boys, whose clothing was marked by, among other things, 'the flamboyant use of colour' (McMillan 2016: 64).

Furthermore, in his other videos, Felmine's choice of clothing is a part of his performance of identity. In the introduction to the Trinidad Bhojpuri series, Felmine notes that the series is inspired by the language of the East Indian indentured labourers, a clear cultural claim. Throughout the series, he dresses in a white headband which has the appearance of a pagri, the headdress associated with East Indian males arriving in Trinidad during indentureship (see Figure 32). Around his neck, Felmine has a set of mala beads, which are prayer beads used in Hinduism, though the white beads are barely visible against his white shirt. Felmine sports a white shirt throughout this series, a clear contrast to the more varied fashion of the first series.

In the Trinidad Patois series, Felmine dons a black T-shirt with red and white lettering: the colours of the national flag of Trinidad and Tobago, as seen in Figure 33. The accompanying video is shown in Video 2.

The T-shirt also contains an outline map of Trinidad and Tobago and a list of Patois sayings, though these are not legible to viewers. Nevertheless, the combination of colours, the outline map, and the sayings are clear indexes of Felmine's national identity, which, in contrast to the identity he espouses in his first series, is now Trinbagonian, that is, including Trinidad *and* Tobago, and not just Trinidadian. In this series, Felmine's headwear deserves special mention. He is wearing a straw hat with a band of plaid red and yellow material tied around it. This style of hat is often worn by singers of folk music and performers of traditional Trinbagonian dances, such as the Belé, in performance. Folk music and dance, and indeed Trinidad Patois, are more often associated with

Figure 33 Felmine in *Patois Letter of the Day* wear (Courtesy Stephon Felmine)

Video 2

Patois Letter of the Day (Courtesy Stephon Felmine) Video file and transcript available at www.cambridge.org/Guyanne

Afro-Trinidadian communities, but it is difficult to ascribe an Afro-Trinidadian identity to Felmine, who is Indo-Trinidadian. Instead, Felmine's choice of dress aligns with the ideal of multiculturalism and national unity purported and promoted in other cultural discourses. This national unity is marked in many ways, one of which is through the adoption of practices historically associated with one ethnic group by other groups within the society, perhaps best encapsulated in the lyrics of the 1996 calypso, *National Unity*, by the Trinidadian calypsonian The Mighty Chalkdust (Hollis Liverpool), in which he comments on the shared practices of different ethnic groups in Trinidad and Tobago and concludes that 'when an African take part in East Indian culture . . . What they are doing, my friend, is pulling races together' (Liverpool, 1996).

3.4 Ideologies in TikTok Videos

In contrast to the memes data, the TikTok videos do not contain any overt ideological statements. The act of creating and posting the videos is an ideological one, since it suggests that the varieties are worthy of documentation. In the video introducing the Trinbago Bhojpuri series, Stephon Felmine tells viewers that 'we ancestors come from so far we can't let them down. We have to keep learning and keep the culture alive', underscoring the ideological stance of this series in particular: the propagation of Indo-Trinidadian language and culture. The videos in this series are presented during the month of May, which culminates in the commemoration of Indian Arrival Day on 30 May, the anniversary of the arrival of the first workers from India on the *Fatel Razak* in Trinidad in 1845.

More frequently, however, ideological work in the *LoD* videos is achieved through intertextuality. Although the TikTokers do not mention other texts in their videos, viewers are quick to make comparisons. Early in Stephon Felmine's series, one commentor draws parallels to *Nelson's West Indian Readers*, posting, 'ABCs like the West Indian Reader yes 😞', and another encourages Felmine to 'make a alphabet chart . . . . no more a for 🍎 (apple) and b for [cricket bat emoji] (bat)', a direct reference to the first page of the *First Primer* of *Nelson's West Indian Readers*, in which the letter A is placed next to a picture of an apple and the letter B next to a picture of a cricket bat (Cutteridge 2014: 2). The first edition of *Nelson's West Indian Readers* appeared in 1927 in response to *Macdougal Readers* and *Royal Readers*, which had no local content (Campbell 1983: 45). The books were intended for use throughout the British West Indies, and an informal survey of parents of four-, five-, and six-year-olds in Barbados and Trinidad during the preparation of this Element suggested that the books are still in use in Infant and Reception classes today. Although

Cutteridge's work did attempt to have more local content, the books were felt to lack relevance and leave their Caribbean readers undereducated. This is perhaps best captured in the lyrics of the song *Dan Is the Man in the Van* (1963) by the Grenadian-Trinidadian calypsonian Mighty Sparrow (Slinger Francisco). The song's title is a direct reference to one of the lessons in the *First Primer* (Cutteridge 2014: 24), which opens with the same lines. In his calypso, Sparrow argues that 'Cutteridge wanted to keep us in ignorance'.

Viewed in light of these discourses, the videos can be understood as responses to colonial and postcolonial education systems. They reject materials and methods originating from the colonial power in favour of local materials and local language. This ideology is encapsulated in user comments such as 'Best. Alphabet. Ever.', which presupposes the existence of less good alphabets, and '😂 [Trinidad and Tobago emoji] ❤💯 d local alphabet 😂', which assumes the existence of non-local alphabets that might receive a score lower than 100. Ideological work of this kind can also be understood within the context of Schneider's (2007) dynamic model of postcolonial English. The model asserts that countries in phase four demonstrate endonormative stabilisation, which involves the acceptance of local norms over external norms. The videos, and the comments accompanying them, promote the use and understanding of local variants and so can be taken as evidence for locating these varieties within phase four of the model.

Another ideology present in the TikTok videos, and one which runs almost counter to the empowering anti-colonial ideology, is the idea of Creole as something funny, not to be taken seriously. Though many commenters note the pedagogical value of the TikTok, the videos are in fact designed to entertain, and the high frequency of acronyms related to humour, such as LOL (laughing out loud) and LMAO (laughing my ass off), and the use of emojis such as the laughing emoji show that they are received as such by the viewers.

3.5 Conclusion

Through their use of a range of linguistic and non-linguistic features, the TikTokers perform elements of their identity and allow users on the platform to make claims and form bonds through affiliation. At a linguistic level, the *LoD* videos entertain and educate by highlighting commonly used vocabulary but also, in the case of Felmine, by introducing lesser-known terms and giving the etymologies of words borrowed into English/Creole. These identity claims take place within a broader context of postcolonial identity formation and the videos' broad circulation (many go into the hundreds of thousands of viewers) and their creators' influencer status suggest both an appetite for and an appreciation of local language varieties in contrast to external norms. At the same time, the ideologies surrounding this identity work are strange bedfellows and see the use of local varieties simultaneously as empowering and entertaining. In the final section of this Element, I explore the processes through which Caribbean Creoles come to be enregistered as indexes of Caribbean identity.

4 Indexing Identity, Enregistering Ideology

4.1 Introduction

The previous sections have demonstrated how linguistic and other semiotic systems contribute to the performance of identity on social media. They also explored how broader ideologies present in Caribbean society inform the content creators' message, as well as the discourse surrounding the content, as seen in the comments and reactions. In this final section, I take the analysis a step further, examining the ways in which the use of language on social media serves to index Caribbean identities and enregister Caribbean Englishes and Creoles and ideologies surrounding their usage.

4.2 Indexing Identity

In many ways, the uses of Creole and English observed in the memes and TikTok videos are no different from earlier accounts of their distribution and usage. Carrington (1999) already established the centrality of Creole in performance domains in the Caribbean: musical genres such as reggae and soca, drama, and oral poetry are all largely performed through Creole. TikTok videos could be considered performances, perhaps a subgenre of the short film, and viewed as such the language use reported in Section 3 is very much in keeping with the expectations of the genre. Similarly, Winer (1993) shows that written representations of Trinidadian Creole are present in hand-drawn comic strips meant as forms of entertainment and social commentary. While memes may be computer-generated, the semiotic resources upon which they draw – words and pictures – are essentially the same as hand-drawn comics, so that here too the use of language maps onto a pattern of language use that has been seen before. Where memes differ from earlier cartoons, however, is in the intertextual nature of the memes, in which meaning is derived in part from understanding and awareness of the ways in which content, form, and stance are similar across groups of memes. Memes rely less on linguistic forms than comic strips do, since a great deal of meaning-making is done through the pictorial element and constant re-contextualisation of existing meme templates.

The findings of this Element show how orders of indexicality are created and maintained in Caribbean contexts. A sign – be it a word, a grammatical form, an intonation pattern, a particular pronunciation – 'is indexical if it is related to its meaning by virtue of co-occurring with the thing it is taken to mean' (Johnstone 2017: 283). In Trinidad in the late 1980s and 1990s, that is, before the era of Google Maps, invitations to children's birthday parties would end with the note: the house with the balloons. Every invitation included it, and so, at least for people coming of age in Trinidad during that period of time, balloons co-occurred with birthday parties, and balloons came to serve as an index of birthday parties so that even if one wasn't invited to a particular birthday party, one could drive past, observe the balloons, and know that a party was, or would soon be, underway. The same thing can happen with language: sounds, words, and phrases can come to signal information about a person's identity – their gender, their socio-economic class, their ethnicity, and their nationality. Not all sounds or words do this in the same way. Johnstone and Kiesling (2008) reconceptualise Silverstein's (2003) orders of indexicality and Labov's (1972) earlier stereotype–marker–indicator system. Johnstone and Kiesling organise orders of indexicality into three levels: first-, second-, and third-order indexicalities. First-order indexicalities are roughly equivalent to Labov's indicator and are linguistic features that are present in the speech of community members but are not used for stylistic variation. Second-order indexicalities are those that do show stylistic variation and whose use is affected by ideologies and discourses surrounding language use, though speakers may not be able to articulate how the features are used themselves. Second-order indexicalities are similar to Labov's marker. Finally, third-order indexicalities map relatively easily onto Labov's stereotype and refer to forms that are readily available for comment and become the focus of talk about language and language use (Johnstone and Kiesling 2008: 9).

All three types of indexicality are present in the Caribbean social media data. Among the first-order indexicalities are those features, such as the glottal stop in the Barbadian TikTok videos and of [a] in LOT contexts in Guyanese videos, which, while they do indicate that the speaker is from Barbados or Guyana, do not do any further indexical work. This is perhaps surprising in the case of the glottal stops, since Blake (2008: 314) seems to imply that the use of glottal stops is a stereotype of Barbadian speech. However, perhaps the key to the apparent inconsistency lies in the fact that Blake links the stereotype in part to the speakers of other Caribbean Creoles and not necessarily Barbadians but Johnstone and Kiesling note that first-order indexicalities are evident to outsiders to the community. Perhaps, then, if a non-Barbadian TikToker was trying to perform a Barbadian accent, they would make a more conscious and stylised use of this feature. In writing, such indicators or first-order indexicalities do not seem to be drawn upon, indeed are not able to be drawn upon, since 'community members have not noticed the first-order indexical correlation between form and demography [. . . and] thus cannot make use of the correlation to interpret others' speech or project social identity' (Johnstone and Kiesling 2008: 10).

In terms of second-order indexicalities, the data shows that several phonetic and phonological features are often instrumentalised in the performance of identity, and that is achieved both in speech and in writing, though it is of course more easily done in speech. Nevertheless, the use of eye dialect spellings in memes to represent pronunciation shows that language users make meaningful use of the sound system of their languages in the performance of their identity. Two phonological variants with which this is done are the stopped and fricative variants of the English voiced and voiceless fricative. The findings of this Element neatly complement Irvine-Sobers's (2018) work on the Jamaican acrolect. She concludes that, for Jamaican speakers, variation in the use of the voiced dental fricative, [ð], and voiced alveolar stop, [d], and the aspirated and palatalised pronunciations of /k/ ([kʰ] and [kj] respectively) are not necessary for demonstrating standardised English speech. Instead, she suggests that speakers exploit these features 'in performing acts of identity or signalling group affiliation' (Irvine-Sobers 2018: 154). Although the linguistic situation of the Caribbean territories studied here is slightly different from the Jamaican one, there are clear parallels to be drawn. All the TikTokers exploit [ð]/[d] and [θ]/[t] variation in their performance of standardised English versus Creole, with the stop variants shouldering greater responsibility in the performance of Caribbean identities, as seen through the concentration of stops versus fricatives in the different sections of the TikTok videos.

The features that become the focus of the memes and TikTok videos are the best candidates to be considered stereotypes or third-order indexicalities, since they are the features around which metapragmatic discourse is centred. Indeed, the videos and memes are inherently metapragmatic and simply the act of their creation becomes a comment on language and language variation in the Caribbean. Lexical items are, in this regard, particularly salient. However, the data shows that even the salience of lexical items is relatively unequal, and some words are better exemplars than others. This is demonstrated when one compares the discourses surrounding the memes and videos. For example, for some words in the *LoD* series, commenters claim lack of familiarity with statements such as 'I learned a new word' or 'He's making up these words'. For other items, however, commenters admit to using them or identify iconic speakers – characterological figures – who make use of the feature, suggesting that some stereotypes are better than others. Silverstein's (2003) original conceptualisation of *nth* and *n+1st* indexical orders foresees the potentiality of infinite orders, but, while adding further levels potentially allows for a more accurate understanding of how indexes are ordered, it could also lead to over-categorisation. Instead, Irvine-Sobers's (2018) notion of load-bearing becomes useful here. Load-bearingness allows for two features to be the subject of metapragmatic discourse, that is, to be considered third-order indexicalities, but for one of them to do more indexical work than the other.

Another issue that becomes apparent through metadiscourse is that members of the speech community may reject or challenge stereotypes. An example of this was seen in the discourse surrounding memes referring to the expression *my one* in Section 2, in which commenters distanced themselves from the form. It will be recalled that this form was particularly associated with South Trinidadian speakers, but several commenters rejected this association, even while reasserting their South Trinidadian identities. Their rejection – and the discourse surrounding it – underlines the dialectic ways surrounding the construction and negotiation of identities online.

Even as some linguistic features are more load-bearing than others, no single feature achieves the work of identity on its own. To return to the balloon analogy one final time: balloons may well signal a birthday party, but a birthday party with just balloons isn't much of a party. Real birthday parties also require cake, treats, presents, and guests. Likewise, the authentic performance of identity requires more than just single words. Indeed, the analysis of both memes and TikTok videos, and the comments surrounding them, has shown that, while individual features, such as words, may come to signal identity, it is not enough to know a lexical item or a phonological feature, to have, as it were, just balloons. Instead, it is the co-occurrence of forms that allows speakers to claim authentic Caribbean identities. These forms include, but are not limited to, linguistic forms, and extend to non-linguistic semiotic markers such as choice of clothing and use of emojis, as has been established for the memes and videos. In this way, the findings here echo Calder's (2019) findings with regard to the performance of gender by drag queens in San Francisco: it is not simply the occurrence of a single feature but rather through 'being situated in a larger semiotic style, it is imbued with social meanings that characterize – and are accomplished by – the entire cross-modal style' (Calder 2019: 346). It is, therefore, not enough to understand the indexical field of a single variable, the 'constellation of ideologically related meanings, any one of which can be activated in the situated use of the variable' (Eckert 2008: 454). It is also necessary to understand how different variants combine in the performance of identity.

4.3 Enregistering Caribbean Englishes and Creoles

Enregisterment refers to 'processes and practices whereby performable signs become recognized (and regrouped) as belonging to distinct, differentially valorized semiotic registers by a population' (Agha 2007: 81). Agha's (2003) early work on the topic traces the means through which Received Pronunciation became historically enregistered as a prestige accent, and later work on enregisterment has demonstrated how linguistic features can become linked to a myriad of language-external features, among them place (e.g. Beal 2009; Johnstone 2013) and social groups. Regarding place, Beal (2009) examines dialect dictionaries and glossaries of the language spoken in Newcastle and Sheffield in the UK from the nineteenth and twentieth centuries and shows how these contribute to the enregisterment of Geordie and Sheffieldish. The data examined in this Element similarly contributes to the enregisterment of Caribbean Englishes and Creoles. Both the *LoD* videos and the memes recording lexical items situate themselves in a history of both lay and linguist codification of Caribbean language. Earlier works such as John Mendes's (1985) *Cote Ci Cote La* (Trinidad), Frank Collymore's (1970) *Notes for a Glossary of Words and Phrases of Barbadian Dialect*, and two 1975 works on Guyanese Creole by A. J. Seymour and C. A. Yansen (Allsopp 2008: 354) represent the impressive efforts by non-linguists to document the vocabulary of Caribbean Creoles. More systematic, scholarly undertakings are represented in large-scale lexicographical projects such as the *Dictionary of Caribbean English Usage* (Allsopp 2003), *The Dictionary of Jamaican English* (Cassidy and Le Page [1967] 2002), and the *Dictionary of the English/Creole* of *Trinidad and Tobago* (Winer 2009). The production and publication of books require considerable time, knowledge, and capital. Engagement with literary materials requires access to books and presupposes a high level of literacy. The relocation of the lexicographical exercise to the digital sphere could be argued to democratise it, since the production and reception of texts are not limited to an elite, educated group. Indeed, the high numbers of views and the frequency of shares suggest broad circulation, no doubt wider than that experienced by printed materials.

Furthermore, Beal (2009: 143) finds that dialect dictionaries enregister 'certain features by claiming them as distinctive of one dialect', even though the features may have been more widespread, and indeed are attested elsewhere. Similar parallels can be found in the *LoD* data, in which TikTokers present lexical items as distinctively Barbadian, Guyanese, or Trinidadian, even though the lexical items exist in other Caribbean Englishes. This was seen in Section 3 through the examples of the words such as *obeah*, *jumbie*, and *horn*, which

TikTokers claim as belonging to Guyanese only, even though they are attested in other varieties. At the same time, Beal shows how the use of nineteenth-century dialect features in twenty-first-century 'indie' music 'consolidates the association of these dialect words with specific localities and the symbolic values attached to them' (Beal 2009: 145). In much the same way, TikTok videos and memes add to the consolidation of the lexical items as markers of Caribbean and/or individual territorial identity. Many of the highlighted lexical items in TikTok videos do in fact appear in glossary lists and within Caribbean dictionaries. Some, such as *kangalang* for Guyanese, *evahsince* for Barbadian, and *quito quito* for Trinidadian, are associated with individual territorial varieties but others are spread more widely. The affiliative claims made in the comments serve to further consolidate the status of lexical items and pronunciation patterns as enregistered markers of Caribbean Englishes and Creoles.

Moreover, TikTok data in particular highlights the ways in which identity becomes enregistered in performance. The Caribbean TikTokers create characterological personae (Agha 2003, 2007) through which identity is performed. Most obviously, this is achieved via their performances, in which Simpson, Wiggins, and Felmine themselves embody the characterological personae associated with the linguistic forms, in much the same way in which Johnstone (2013) shows how Pittsburghese is embodied and enacted through the radio hosts and their use of the /aw/ diphthong, a stereotypical feature of Pittsburgh speech. Johnstone has furthermore demonstrated how Pittsburghese is enregistered through its commodification – the creation of Yinz mementos such as T-shirts (Johnstone 2013: 175) and the Yappin' Yinzer dolls. Ostensibly, no similar material products – in the sense of tangible goods – seem to be produced by the social media content creators, though such products are sold by other agencies not discussed in this Element. At the same time, I would argue that, in making themselves the characterological figures with whom their respective varieties can be associated, the TikTokers market themselves in much the same way the creators of the Yappin' Yinzer dolls market Chipped Ham Sam and Nebbie Debbie (Johnstone 2013). This seems true for both Kwame Simpson and Stephon Felmine, who go on to enjoy considerable material success. Felmine, for instance, is subsequently seen in several advertisements, in which the *LoD* format is drawn upon to sell products. Characterological personae are not limited to the TikTok videos, however. They are also part of the memes. In establishing groups such as Trinis, Convent Girls, South people, Guyanese, and Venezuelans, as explored in Section 2, the creators of memes link 'differences of [language] to matters of social identity' (Agha 2003: 251), where the naming of distinct groups, as Convent Girls and Hindu Convent Girls is similar to the 'minutely differentiated characterological figures' that Agha (2003: 260) identifies.

Enregisterment is concerned not only with which features become enregistered but also with the processes through which language and ideologies surrounding language use spread. Agha argues that this takes place through speech chains, in which ideas about language are passed from speaker to speaker, with speakers able to be both sender and receiver of the ideologies passed along the chain. Critically, Agha (2003: 249) notes that '18th and 19th century metadiscourses ... transmit ideas about accent through print artefacts – books, manuals, magazines, newspapers, etc. – that can be read at different times by different persons'. In twenty-first-century digital contexts, memes and videos replace, or at least serve alongside, other forms of print, audio, and video artefacts in the circulation of language ideologies. This is seen, in part, through the sheer number of times that videos have been viewed and shared; some *LoD* videos received more than 100,000 views via the TikTok platform alone. This doesn't include views on other platforms such as Facebook, YouTube, or Instagram, where the video was also shared. Contemporary digital media accelerates the rate at which ideas about language use are circulated, and the participatory nature of online platforms such as Facebook and TikTok means that these ideas are created and recreated collaboratively, as Chau (2021) also asserted in her discussion of ideologies surrounding ABC speakers.

4.4 Closing Thoughts

The roots of this Element lie in the ludic; I was initially amused and entertained by memes about *curry chicken* and *chicken curry.* Indeed, as Deumert (2014: 27) notes, self-presentation on social media involves appearing 'light-hearted and creative, enjoyable and full of possibilities'. Deumert's paper focusses on the carnivalesque nature of language on social media, a metaphor that is also apt for understanding Caribbean social media, and in particular the use of memes in Trinidad, where Carnival, with its constant juxtaposition of rebellion and revelry, is a core part of national identity. However, whereas Deumert's data and analysis underscore parody and play, the Trinidadian memes show that humour may at times be underpinned by discrimination, xenophobia, and exclusion. Furthermore, when Schneider (2016: 280) highlighted the potential of YouTube, he noted that the platform could be useful for 'studies of language attitudes, laypeople's knowledge of language, or the interaction between culture and language'. Few studies of World Englishes on the web have exploited this particular potential, with scholars preferring to use YouTube as a resource for the description of World Englishes. This is important work, but, if World Englishes is to discourse with other related disciplines, and especially if World Englishes scholarship is to close the growing gap between itself and sociolinguistics more broadly (Saraceni 2017), then it is imperative that scholarship in World Englishes moves beyond the description of features and varieties and engages with sociolinguistic theory, with the ways in which features are drawn upon to index aspects of identity, the ideologies underlying their use, and the ways in which they become enregistered. This is what I have attempted to do. At the same time, the present Element demonstrates that the notion of the national variety, so central to World Englishes, is still both relevant and necessary. For, even as users are involved in hybrid uses of language that involve 'the use of linguistic resources without nationally defined artificial borders' (Saraceni 2017: 120), they are also using language online to create a sense of place. Nowhere is this more evident than in the TikTok videos and the comments attached to them. Here, TikTokers often draw on shared information contexts to create authentic, if imagined, physical contexts. In doing so, they attend to the sense of nostalgia – from the Greek *nostos*, meaning homecoming, and *algia*, pain – upon which their viewers' affiliations are built and within which performances of identity can take place.

References

Agha, A. (2003). The social life of cultural value. *Language & Communication*, 23(3–4), 231–273. https://doi.org/10.1016/S0271-5309(03)00012-0.

Agha, A. (2005). Voice, footing, enregisterment. *Journal of Linguistic Anthropology*, 15(1), 38–59. https://doi.org/10.1525/jlin.2005.15.1.38.

Agha, A. (2007). *Language and Social Relations*. New York: Cambridge University Press. https://doi.org/10.1017/CBO9780511618284.

Alleyne, M. C. (1971). Acculturation and the cultural matrix of creolization. In D. Hymes, ed., *Pidginization and Creolization of Languages*. Cambridge: Cambridge University Press, 169–186.

Allsopp, J. (2008). Dictionaries of Caribbean English. In A. P. Cowie, ed., *The Oxford History of English Lexicography*. Oxford: Clarendon Press, 353–377.

Allsopp, R. (2003). *Dictionary of Caribbean English Usage*. Mona: University of the West Indies Press.

Androutsopoulos, J. (2015). Networked multilingualism: Some language practices on Facebook and their implications. *International Journal of Bilingualism*, 19(2), 185–205. https://doi.org/10.1177/1367006913489198.

Androutsopoulos, J. (2017). Online data collection. In C. Mallinson, B. Childs, and G. Van Herk, eds., *Data Collection in Sociolinguistics*. London: Routledge, 233–244.

Beal, J. C. (2009). Enregisterment, commodification, and historical context: 'Geordie' versus 'Sheffieldish'. *American Speech*, 84(2), 138–156. https://doi.org/10.1215/00031283-2009-012.

Behnken, B. D. and Smithers, G. D. (2015). *Racism in American Popular Media: From Aunt Jemima to the Frito Bandito*. Santa Barbara, CA: Bloomsbury Publishing USA.

Beninger, K. (2016). Social media users' views on the ethics of social media research. In L. Sloan and A. Quan-Haase, eds., *The SAGE Handbook of Social Media Research Methods*. London: SAGE Publications, 57–73. https://doi.org/10.4135/9781473983847.

Bhatia, A. (2020). Vlogging and the discursive co-construction of ethnicity and beauty. *World Englishes*, 39(1), 7–21. https://doi.org/10.1111/weng.12442

Bickerton, D. (1975). *Dynamics of a Creole System*. London: Cambridge University Press.

Blake, R. (1997). All o'we is one? Race, class, and language in a Barbados community. Unpublished PhD dissertation, Stanford University.

Blake, R. (2008). Bajan: Phonology. In E. Schneider, ed., *Varieties of English, Vol. 2: The Americas and the Caribbean*. Berlin: De Gruyter Mouton, 312–319. https://doi.org/10.1515/9783110208405.1.312.

Bohmann, A. (2016). 'Nobody canna cross it': Language-ideological dimensions of hypercorrect speech in Jamaica. *English Language & Linguistics*, 20 (1), 129–152. https://doi:10.1017/S1360674315000374.

Brereton, B. (2010). The historical background to the culture of violence in Trinidad Tobago. *Caribbean Review of Gender studies*, 4, 1–15.

Brown, D. C. (2009). Parang side coming: The 'color' and 'sound' of Trinidad's 'Spanish' heritage. Unpublished PhD dissertation, New York University.

Bucholtz, M. and Hall, K. (2005). Identity and interaction: A sociocultural linguistic approach. *Discourse Studies*, 7(4–5), 585–614. https://doi.org/10.1177/1461445605054407.

Calder, J. (2019). From sissy to sickening: The indexical landscape of /s/ in SoMa, San Francisco. *Journal of Linguistic Anthropology*, 29(3), 332–358. https://doi.org/10.1111/jola.12218.

Campbell, C. C. (1983). Education and black consciousness: The Amazing Captain J. O. Cutteridge in Trinidad and Tobago, 1921–42. *The Journal of Caribbean History*, 18(1), 35–66.

Cape, R. and Stewart, D. (2009). Tusty. On *Soca Gold 2009*. Port of Spain: VP Records.

Carrington, L. D. (1999). The status of Creole in the Caribbean. *Caribbean Quarterly*, 45(2–3), 41–51. https://doi.org/10.1080/00086495.1999.11829615.

Cassidy, F. G., and Le Page, R. B. (Robert B. [1967] 2002. *Dictionary of Jamaican English*. Cambridge: Cambridge University Press.

Cathala, X., Ocho, O. N., Mcintosh, N., Watts, P. N., and Moorley, C. (2022). An exploration of social participation in Caribbean student nurses' use of social media in their learning journey. *Journal of Advanced Nursing*, 79(8), 2900–2910. https://doi.org/10.1111/jan.15499.

Chau, D. (2021). Spreading language ideologies through social media: Enregistering the 'fake ABC' variety in Hong Kong. *Journal of Sociolinguistics*, 25(4), 596–616. https://doi.org/10.1111/josl.12486.

Collister, L. B. (2011). *-repair in online discourse. *Journal of Pragmatics*, 43(3), 918–921. https://doi.org/10.1016/j.pragma.2010.09.025.

Coupland, N. (2007). *Style: Language Variation and Identity*. Cambridge: Cambridge University Press. https://doi.org/10.1017/CBO9780511755064.

Cutteridge, J. (2014). *Nelson's West Indian Readers First Primer*, Vol. 1. London: Nelson Thornes.

DeCamp, D. (1971). Toward a generative analysis of a post-creole speech continuum. In D. Hymes, ed., *Pidginization and Creolization of Languages*. Cambridge: Cambridge University Press, 347–370.

Denisova, A. (2019). *Internet Memes and Society: Social, Cultural, and Political Contexts*. London: Routledge. https://doi.org/10.4324/9780429469404.

Deuber, D. (2009). Standard English in the secondary school in Trinidad. In T. Hoffman and L. Siebers, eds., *World Englishes – Problems, Properties and Prospects: Selected Papers from the 13th IAWE Conference*. Amsterdam: John Benjamins, 83–104. https://doi.org/10.1075/veaw.g40.

Deuber, D., Hänsel, E. C., and Westphal, M. (2021). Quotative be like in Trinidadian English. *World Englishes*, 40(3), 436–458. https://doi.org/10.1111/weng.12465.

Deuber, D. and Leung, G. A. (2013). Investigating attitudes towards an emerging standard of English: Evaluations of newscasters' accents in Trinidad. *Multilingua – Journal of Cross-Cultural and Interlanguage Communication*, 32(3), 289–319. https://doi.org/10.1515/multi-2013-0014.

Deumert, A. (2014). *Sociolinguistics and Mobile Communication*. Edinburgh: Edinburgh University Press. https://doi.org/10.1515/9780748655755.

Devonish, H. and Thomas, E. A. (2012). Standards of English in the Caribbean. In R. Hickey, ed., *Standards of English: Codified Varieties around the World*. Cambridge: Cambridge University Press, 179–197. https://doi.org/10.1017/CBO9781139023832.

Durham, M. (2016). Changing attitudes towards the Welsh English accent: A view from Twitter. In M. Durham and J. Morris, eds., *Sociolinguistics in Wales*. Cham: Palgrave Macmillan, 181–205. https://doi.org/10.1057/978-1-137-52897-1.

Eckert, P. (2008). Variation and the indexical field. *Journal of Sociolinguistics*, 12(4), 453–476.

Ehrlich, A. S. (1971). History, ecology, and demography in the British Caribbean: An analysis of East Indian ethnicity. *Southwestern Journal of Anthropology*, 27(2), 166–180.

Esposito, E. (2018). The social media campaign for Caribbean reparations: A critical multimodal investigation. In E. Esposito, C. Pérez-Arredondo, and J. M. Ferreiro, eds., *Discourses from Latin America and the Caribbean: Current Concepts and Challenges*. Cham: Palgrave Macmillan, 175–209. https://doi.org/10.1007/978-3-319-93623-9.

Felix, J. J. (2020). Culture jamming in the Caribbean: A case of alternative media through double alternativity in Trinidad and Tobago. *Archipelagos: A Journal of Caribbean Digital Praxis*, (5). https://doi.org/10.7916/archipelagos-fx7k-bj27.

Fenigsen, J. (2003). Language ideologies in Barbados: Processes and paradigms. *Pragmatics: Quarterly Publication of the International Pragmatics Association (IPrA)*, 13(4), 457–481.

Ferreira, J.-A. and Heitmeier, K.-A. (2015). 'A description of Trinidadian pronunciation.' Society for Caribbean Linguistics Occasional Paper No. 42.

Francisco, S. (1963). Dan is the man in the van. On *Harry and Mama/Dan is the Man in the Van*. Jamaica: West Indian Record Label.

Goffman, E. (1979). Footing. *Semiotica*, 25(1–2), 1–30. https://doi.org/10.1515/semi.1979.25.1-2.1.

Gooden, S. and Drayton, K. A. (2017). The Caribbean. In R. Hickey, ed., *Listening to the Past: Audio Records of Accents of English*. Cambridge: Cambridge University Press, 414–443.

Hackert, S. (2016). Standards of English in the Caribbean. In E. Seoane and C. Suárez-Gómez, eds., *World Englishes: New Theoretical and Methodological Considerations*. Amsterdam: John Benjamins, 85–111. https://doi.org/10.1075/veaw.g57.

Hackert, S. and Deuber, D. (2015). American influence on written Caribbean English. In P. Collins, ed., *Grammatical Change in English World-Wide*, Amsterdam: John Benjamins, 389–410. https://doi.org/10.1075/scl.67.

Hänsel, E. C. and Meer, P. (2023). Comparing attitudes toward Caribbean, British, and American accents in Trinidad and Tobago, the United Kingdom, and the United States. *World Englishes*, 42(1), 130–149. https://doi.org/10.1111/weng.12618.

Hänsel, E. C., Westphal, M., Meer, P., and Deuber, D. (2022). Context matters: Grenadian students' attitudes toward newscasters' and teachers' accents. *Journal of Pidgin and Creole Languages*, 37(1), 16–52. https://doi.org/10.1075/jpcl.00085.han.

Haynes, L. (1982). Rural and urban groups in Barbados and Guyana: Language attitudes and behaviors. *International Journal of the Sociology of Language*, 1982(34), 67–82. https://doi.org/10.1515/ijsl.1982.34.67.

Hinrichs, L. and White-Sustaíta, J. (2011). Global Englishes and the sociolinguistics of spelling: A study of Jamaican blog and email writing. *English World-Wide*, 32(1), 46–73. https://doi.org/10.1075/eww.32.1.03hin.

Holm, J. (1986). The spread of English in the Caribbean area. In M. Görlach and J. Holm, eds., *Focus on the Caribbean*. Amsterdam: John Benjamins, 1–22. https://doi.org/10.1075/veaw.g8.

Honkanen, M. (2020). *World Englishes on the Web: The Nigerian Diaspora in the USA*. Amsterdam: John Benjamins. https://doi.org/10.1075/veaw.g63.

Honkanen, M. and Müller, J. (2021). Interjections and emojis in Nigerian online communication. *World Englishes*, 40(4), 611–630. https://doi.org/10.1111/weng.12544.

Ilbury, C. (2023). The recontextualisation of Multicultural London English: Stylising the 'roadman'. *Language in Society*, 1–25. https://doi:10.1017/S0047404523000143.

Ilona, A. (2005). 'Laughing through the tears': Mockery and self-representation in VS Naipaul's *A House for Mr Biswas* and Earl Lovelace's *The Dragon Can't Dance*. In S. Reichl and M. Stein, eds., *Cheeky Fictions*. Leiden: Brill, 43–60.

Irvine-Sobers, G. A. (2018). *The Acrolect in Jamaica: The Architecture of Phonological Variation*. Berlin: Language Science Press. https://doi.org/10.5281/zenodo.1306618.

James, W. and Youssef, V. (2008). The creoles of Trinidad and Tobago: Morphology and syntax. In E. Schneider, eds., *Varieties of English, Vol. 2: The Americas and the Caribbean*. Berlin: De Gruyter Mouton, 661–692. https://doi.org/10.1515/9783110208405.2.661.

Johnstone, B. (2013). *Speaking Pittsburghese: The Story of a Dialect*. Oxford: Oxford University Press.

Johnstone, B. (2017). Characterological figures and expressive style in the enregisterment of linguistic variety. In C. Montgomery and E. Moore, eds., *Language and a Sense of Place: Studies in Language and Region*. Cambridge: Cambridge University Press, 283–300. https://doi.org/10.1017/9781316162477.

Johnstone, B. and Kiesling, S. F. (2008). Indexicality and experience: Exploring the meanings of /aw/-monophthongization in Pittsburgh. *Journal of Sociolinguistics*, 12, 5–33. https://doi.org/10.1111/j.1467-9841.2008.00351.x.

Jones, J. M. and Liverpool, H. V. (1976). Calypso humour in Trinidad. In A. J. Chapman and H. C Foot, eds., *Humor and Laughter: Theory, Research, and Applications*. London: Routledge, 259–286.

Jovanovic, D. and Van Leeuwen, T. (2018). Multimodal dialogue on social media. *Social Semiotics*, 28(5), 683–699. https://doi.org/10.1080/10350330.2018.1504732.

Kathpalia, S. S. (2023). Satiric parody through Indian English tweets in Twitter. *World Englishes*, 42, 606–623. https://doi.org/10.1111/weng.12579.

Kerrigan, D. (2016). Languaculture and grassroots football: 'Small goal' in Trinidad. *International Review for the Sociology of Sport*, 51(6), 735–751. https://doi.org/10.1177/1012690214552431.

Kress, G. R. (2010). *Multimodality: A Social Semiotic Approach to Contemporary Communication*. London: Taylor & Francis.

Labov, W. (1972). *Sociolinguistic Patterns*. Philadelphia: University of Pennsylvania Press.

Lacoste, V. (2013). The Caribbean. In M. Filppula, J. Klemola, and D. Sharma, eds., *The Oxford Handbook of World Englishes*. Oxford: Oxford Handbooks, 389–408. https://doi.org/10.1093/oxfordhb/9780199777716.013.39.

Le Page, R. B. and Tabouret-Keller, A. (1985). *Acts of Identity: Creole-Based Approaches to Language and Ethnicity*. Cambridge: Cambridge University Press.

Leung, G. A. (2013). A synchronic sociophonetic study of monophthongs in Trinidadian English. PhD dissertation, University of Freiburg.

Leung, G. A. (2017). YouTube comments as metalanguage data on non-standardized languages: The case of Trinidadian Creole English in soca music. In S Hai-Jew, ed., *Data Analytics in Digital Humanities: Multimedia Systems and Applications*. New York: Springer, 231–250. https://doi.org/10.1007/978-3-319-54499-1_10.

Leung, G. A. and Deuber, D. (2014). Indo-Trinidadian speech: An investigation into a popular stereotype surrounding pitch. In M. Hundt and D. Sharma, eds., *English in the Indian Diaspora*. Amsterdam: John Benjamins, 9–27. https://doi.org/10.1075/veaw.g50.

Liverpool, H. (1996). National unity. YouTube video. Posted July 26, 2008. www.youtube.com/watch?v=dksgypdvsoQ. Last accessed 17 January 2024.

Mahabir, C. (1996). Wit and popular music: The calypso and the blues. *Popular Music*, 15(1), 55–81. https://10.1017/S0261143000007960.

Mair, C. (2013). The world system of Englishes: Accounting for the transnational importance of mobile and mediated vernaculars. *English World-Wide*, 34(3), 253–278. https://doi.org/10.1075/eww.34.3.01mai.

Maynard, D. M. B. and Jules, M. A. (2021). Exploring her roots: Black Caribbean hair identity and going natural using social media networks. *Journal of Black Psychology*, 47(1), 3–30. https://doi.org/10.1177/0095798420971892.

McMillan, M. (2016). Saga bwoys and rude bwoys: Migration, grooming, and dandyism. *Journal of Contemporary African Art*, 2016(38–39), 60–69. https://doi.org/10.1215/10757163-3641689.

Meer, P. and Fuchs, R. (2022). The Trini sing-song: Sociophonetic variation in Trinidadian English prosody and differences to other varieties. *Language and Speech*, 65(4), 923–957. https://doi.org/10.1177/0023830921998404.

Meer, P., Westphal, M., Hänsel, E. C., and Deuber, D. (2019). Trinidadian secondary school students' attitudes toward accents of Standard English.

Journal of Pidgin and Creole Languages, 34(1), 83–125. https://doi.org/10.1075/jpcl.00029.mee.

Miller, D. and Sinanan, J. (2017). *Visualising Facebook: A Comparative Perspective*. London: UCL Press.

Mohammed, S. N. and Thombre, A. (2017). An investigation of user comments on Facebook pages of Trinidad and Tobago's Indian music format radio stations. *Journal of Radio & Audio Media*, 24(1), 111–129. https://doi.org/10.1080/19376529.2016.1252374.

Moll, A. (2015). *Jamaican Creole Goes Web*. Amsterdam: John Benjamins. https://doi.org/10.1075/cll.49.

Mortensen, M. and Neumayer, C. (2021). The playful politics of memes. *Information, Communication & Society*, 24(16), 2367–2377. https://10.1080/1369118X.2021.1979622.

Mühleisen, S. (2001). Is 'bad English' dying out? A diachronic comparative study of attitudes towards Creole versus Standard English in Trinidad. *Philologie im Netz*, 2001(15), 43–78.

Mühleisen, S. (2022). *Genre in World Englishes: Case Studies from the Caribbean*. Amsterdam: John Benjamins. https://doi.org/10.1075/veaw.g67.

Rickford, J. R. (1987). *Dimensions of a Creole Continuum: History, Texts, and Linguistic Analysis of Guyanese Creole*. Stanford, CA: Stanford University Press.

Saraceni, M. (2017). World Englishes and linguistic border crossings. In E. Ling Low and A. Pakir, eds., *World Englishes: Rethinking Paradigms*. London: Routledge, 154–171.

Schneider, E. W. (2007). *Postcolonial English: Varieties around the world*. Cambridge: Cambridge University Press. https://doi.org/10.1017/CBO9780511618901.

Schneider, E. W. (2016). World Englishes on YouTube. In E. Seoane and C. Suárez-Gómez, eds., *World Englishes: New Theoretical and Methodological Considerations*, Amsterdam: John Benjamins: 253–282.

Shakir, M. (2023). Functions of code-switching in online registers of Pakistani English. In G. Wilson and M. Westphal, eds., *New Englishes, New Methods*, Amsterdam: John Benjamins, 42–64. https://doi.org/10.1075/veaw.g68.

Shaw, C., Stuart, J., Thomas, T., and Kolves, K. (2022). Suicidal behaviour and ideation in Guyana: A systematic literature review. *The Lancet Regional Health–Americas*, (11), 2–11. https://doi.org/10.1016/j.lana.2022.100253.

Shifman, L. (2014). The cultural logic of photo-based meme genres. *Journal of Visual Culture*, 13(3), 340–358. https://doi.org/10.1177/1470412914546577.

Sidnell, J. (1999). Gender and pronominal variation in an Indo-Guyanese creole-speaking community. *Language in Society*, 28(3), 367–399. https://doi.org/10.1017/S0047404599003036.

Silverstein, M. (2003). Indexical order and the dialectics of sociolinguistic life. *Language & Communication*, 23(3–4), 193–229. https://doi.org/10.1016/S0271-5309(03)00013-2.

Sinanan, J. (2017). *Social Media in Trinidad: Values and Visibility*. London: UCL Press.

Singh, K. (2023). 'I know the world by how I speak the world': TikTok ABCs, disaster language and Andre Salkey's *Hurricane*. *Archipelagos: A Journal of Caribbean Digital Praxis*, (7), 1–20. https://10.7916/archipelagos-0704.

Smith, T. and Short, A. (2022). Needs affordance as a key factor in likelihood of problematic social media use: Validation, latent profile analysis and comparison of TikTok and Facebook problematic use measures. *Addictive Behaviors*, 129, 1–11. https://doi.org/10.1016/j.addbeh.2022.107259.

Spilioti, T. (2020). The weirding of English, trans-scripting, and humour in digital communication. *World Englishes*, 39(1), 106–118. https://doi.org/10.1111/weng.12450.

Stell, G. (2018). Representing variation in creole continua: A folk linguistic view of language variation in Trinidad. *Journal of English Linguistics*, 46(2), 113–139. https://doi.org/10.1177/0075424218769724.

Stuka, C. (2023). The Americanization of Barbadian English. *World Englishes*, 42(1), 91–114.

Unuabonah, F. O. and Oyebode, O. O. (2021). 'Nigeria is fighting Covid-419': A multimodal critical discourse analysis of political protest in Nigerian coronavirus-related internet memes. *Discourse & Communication*, 15(2), 200–219. https://doi.org/10.1177/1750481320982090.

Van Leeuwen, T. and Kress, G. (1995). Critical layout analysis. *Internationale Schulbuchforschung*, 17(1), 25–43.

Wainwright, L. (2022). A new paradigm, moving on from Bakhtin. *Journal of Festival Culture Inquiry and Analysis*, 1(1), 28–32.

Wiggins, B. E. (2019). *The Discursive Power of Memes in Digital Culture: Ideology, Semiotics, and Intertextuality*. New York: Routledge.

Wilson, G. (2023). British and American norms in the Trinidadian English lexicon. *World Englishes*, 42(1), 73–90. https://doi.org/10.1111/weng.12609.

Wilson, M. (2023). The value of ethnographic research for sustainable diet interventions: Connecting old and new foodways in Trinidad. *Sustainability*, 15(6), 5383. https://doi.org/10.3390/su15065383.

Winer, L. (2009). *Dictionary of the English/Creole of Trinidad and Tobago: On Historical Principles*. Montreal: McGill-Queen's Press.

Winer, L. (1993). *Trinidad and Tobago*. Amsterdam: John Benjamins. https://doi.org/10.1075/veaw.t6.

Winford, D. (1976). Teacher attitudes toward language varieties in a creole community. *International Journal of the Sociology of Language*, 1976(8), 45–76. https://doi.org/10.1515/ijsl.1976.8.45.

Winford, D. (1978). Phonological hypercorrection in the process of decreolization: The case of Trinidadian English. *Journal of Linguistics*, 14(2), 277–291.

Winford, D. (1997). Re-examining Caribbean English creole continua. *World Englishes*, 16(2), 233–279.

Youssef, V. (2004). 'Is English we speaking': Trinbagonian in the twenty-first century. *English Today*, 20(4), 42–49. https://10.1017/S0266078404004080.

Youssef, V. and James, W. (2008). The creoles of Trinidad and Tobago: Phonology. In B. Kortmann and E. Schneider, eds.,*Varieties of English, Vol. 2: The Americas and the Caribbean*. Berlin: De Gruyter Mouton, 320–338. https://doi.org/10.1515/9783110208405.1.320.

Yus, F. (2018). Identity-related issues in meme communication. *Internet Pragmatics*, 1(1), 113–133.

Zähres, F. (2021). Broadcasting your variety. In A. Schroeder, ed., *The Dynamics of English in Namibia: Perspectives on an Emerging Variety*. Amsterdam: John Benjamins, 135–168. https://doi.org/10.1075/veaw.g65.

Zappavigna, M. (2011). Ambient affiliation: A linguistic perspective on Twitter. *New Media & Society*, 13(5), 788–806. https://doi.org/10.1177/1461444810385097.

Acknowledgements

I would like to thank two anonymous reviewers for their thorough and generous reading of an earlier version of this Element, as well as the series editor Edgar W. Schneider, for his patience and guidance. I am much indebted to the following people: Michelle Tardieu-Attale for explanations of traditional clothing; Jakob Leimgruber, Sven Leuckert, and Sofia Rüdiger for the conference workshop at ISLE 2021, where Section 2 was first presented; Michael Westphal and Muhammad Shakir for reading earlier versions of Section 2; the participants of the University of Westminster Forum on Language and Linguistics research series in March 2023 and the attendees of the Quirk Symposium at the British Academy in June 2023 for their kind feedback on lecture versions of Sections 3 and 4; Charlotte Roberts and Linda Freedman for discussions on the notion of home, place, and the etymology of *nostalgia*; and everyone who has ever sent me a meme or a video via social media.

Cambridge Elements

World Englishes

About the Series

Over the last centuries, the English language has spread all over the globe due to a multitude of factors including colonization and globalization. In investigating these phenomena, the vibrant linguistic sub-discipline of "World Englishes" has grown substantially, developing appropriate theoretical frameworks and considering applied issues. This Elements series will cover all the topics of the discipline in an accessible fashion and will be supplemented by on-line material.

Cambridge Elements ☰

World Englishes

Elements in the Series

Uniformity and Variability in the Indian English Accent
Caroline R. Wiltshire

Posthumanist World Englishes
Lionel Wee

The Cognitive Foundation of Post-colonial Englishes: Construction Grammar as the Cognitive Theory for the Dynamic Model
Thomas Hoffmann

Inheritance and Innovation in the Evolution of Rural African American English
Guy Bailey, Patricia Cukor-Avila and Juan Salinas

Indian Englishes in the Twenty-First Century: Unity and Diversity in Lexicon and Morphosyntax
Sven Leuckert, Claudia Lange, Tobias Bernaisch and Asya Yurchenko

Language Ideologies and Identities on Facebook and TikTok: A Southern Caribbean Perspective
Guyanne Wilson

A full series listing is available at: www.cambridge.org/EIWE

Printed in the United States
by Baker & Taylor Publisher Services